Yasser and Zahra Experience the Hajj

In the Name of Allah, the Kind, the Merciful

With special thanks to Shaykh Muhammad Saeed Bahmanpoor for checking the work for accuracy of Islamic History and interpretation, and to Fatma Ali Jaffer for her outstanding editing.

Published by
Sun Behind The Cloud Publications Ltd
PO Box 15889, Birmingham, B16 6NZ
This edition first published in paperback 2024
Text copyright © Sun Behind The Cloud 2024
The moral rights of the authors have been asserted
All rights reserved
A CIP catalogue record for this book is available from the British Library
ISBN (print): 978-1-908110-91-6
ISBN (ebook): 978-1-908110-92-3
www.sunbehindthecloud.com
info@sunbehindthecloud.com

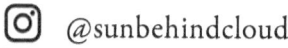 @sunbehindcloud

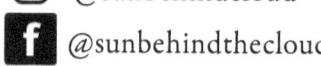 @sunbehindthecloud

قَدْ كَانَتْ لَكُمْ أُسْوَةٌ حَسَنَةٌ فِيْ إِبْرَاهِيْمَ وَالَّذِيْنَ مَعَهُ

*You already have an excellent example in
Abraham and those with him (60:4)*

Share your Learning with Yasser and Zahra

If you would like to take part in some of our crafts and activities, you can download them from our website:

https://www.sunbehindthecloud.com/share-your-learning-with-yasser-and-zahra

If you would like to send a personal message to Yasser and Zahra, you can email them on:

yasserandzahra@sunbehindthecloud.com

We're looking forward to hearing from you!

Contents

Shahr Ramadhan   p8

Shawwal   p19

Dhul Qa'dah   p27

Dhul Hijjah   P34

dear reader,

Are you ready for another adventure with Yasser and Zahra? This time, we are off to Makkah to experience the Hajj! Hajj is a pilgrimage which is wajib (obligatory) on every single Muslim, (so long as they can afford it).

Whilst you are still young, (and saving up your pocket money), you can travel on Grandfather's time-travelling rug to meet Prophet Ibrahim and his blessed family. You'll find out what it means to truly worship One God, and trust Him completely! The book you are holding is guaranteed to take you on an adventure you will never forget!

So buckle up and get ready for the ride! Remember that the characters - Yasser, Zahra and Grandfather - and their means of travel are all fictional. However, the prophets and holy personalities that they meet and all their stories, are true facts of history, many of which are recorded in the Holy Qur'an!

Did you know that there are about two hundred and forty five verses of the Qur'an that refer to Prophet Ibrahim? Next time you are reading our holy book, try to listen out for his name!

It is our deepest hope that after reading this book, you reflect on the lessons you have learnt and try to live in the way of Prophet Ibrahim every day!

$$رَبَّنَا تَقَبَّلْ مِنَّا$$

$$اِنَّكَ اَنْتَ السَّمِيْعُ الْعَلِيْمُ$$

*"Our Lord! Accept [this] from us.
You are indeed the All-Hearing, All-Knowing..."*

Prophet Ibrahim and Prophet Ismael's prayer found in Surah Baqarah, verse 127.

Shahr ramadhan

Chapter 1

The aroma of freshly fried samosas wafted up the stairs. In his room, Yasser inhaled deeply and his belly responded with a low growl, like a baby bear was trapped inside of it. What he really wanted in his tummy was one of those samosas…or maybe two, or three…he imagined the crunch when he bit into one of those yummy triangles and his mouth began to water. He quickly wrapped his arms around himself and looked at the clock on the wall. Not long to go. He decided to go check on Zahra and see what she was up to.

"MMMM, CAN YOU SMELL THAT?" Yasser walked into his sister's room and threw himself dramatically on her rug. When she didn't respond, he looked around to see what she was doing.

Zahra was busy at her desk, looking at a checklist of things to do in the last ten nights of Ramadhan. "Ghusl? Done. Charity?" She put her hand in her pocket. "Got it," she said, holding up a silver coin. "Everything is on track!" She finally turned to Yasser. "Sorry, what were you saying?"

"THE SAMOSAS!" Yasser exclaimed as if Zahra needed to get her priorities straight. "It's almost Maghrib time and I'm starving! These last few days of fasting are the hardest!"

"No way!" Zahra said. "It gets easier every day!"

Yasser's grumbling tummy wasn't convinced. "At the end of Ramadhan, I feel like I've got the hunger from all the other days added up inside me!"

"That's not how it works! With every day that you fast, your body gets more and more used to being without food. Remember how weird it feels to have lunch on Eid day?"

"Well, it doesn't sound like you're hungry at all!" Yasser retorted. "I guess all the samosas are for me then!"

Zahra chuckled but made a mental note to get to the dinner table on time. She didn't really mind Yasser eating all the samosas as long as there was dessert! Zahra was a sweet tooth and her mother often teased her that she could survive on ice cream and jelly beans alone if she was allowed to.

"ALLAHU AKBAR!" Grandfather's melodious voice rang out, reaching all the corners of the house.

It was time for Maghrib prayers and the end of a long day of fasting. After what felt like three of the longest rakaats (Grandfather enjoyed reciting his favourite surahs in the last nights of Ramadhan), Yasser rushed to the dinner table spread with samosas, spicy rice, and comforting cups of sweet tea. Zahra shook her head and followed Grandfather and Mum, matching their more reasonable pace.

Once they had all sat down, Mum recited the fast-breaking prayer, **"O ALLAH, FOR YOU I FAST, AND WITH THE FOOD YOU GIVE ME I BREAK THE FAST, AND I RELY ON YOU."** Then they all broke their fasts as a family.

For Yasser, it was dates first, followed by some water and then ten of the crunchy samosas he had been dreaming about. When he was done, he sat back in his chair with a satisfied smile. "Alhamdullilah!"

Grandfather smiled back. "Did you know that there are two rewards for the person who fasts?" He did not wait for a reply. "The first is the iftar," he said, pointing to the empty plate of samosas.

"What could be better than that?" Yasser asked, with a sigh of contentment.

"The second reward is waiting for us in Heaven!" Grandfather said.

"Allah is most Generous..." Mum said, almost to herself.

As soon as everyone had finished eating, Grandfather and Mum put away the food while Yasser and Zahra helped to clear up and load the dishwasher. They all moved quickly with an excited sense of energy. It was an extremely precious night that had started with the setting of the sun. Millions of angels were already descending to fill the earth because tonight was a night of promised blessings and answered prayers; a night better than a thousand months! It was Laylatul Qadr and they didn't want to waste a single moment of it!

Once the iftar was cleared, each of them went to freshen up, perform wudhu, collect their prayer books and copies of the Holy Qur'an. Grandfather even let Yasser wear some of his favourite rose perfume, although Yasser secretly preferred the smell of samosas.

"I'm waiting at the door!" Mum was the first one ready.

Grandfather and Yasser quickly appeared and began lacing up their shoes.

"Zahra! Where are you?" Mum called out. "We're going to be late!"

"Coming! Coming!" Zahra rummaged in a panic around her room. She knew she had put the list of all her family and friends to include in her du'as somewhere safe, but where? She finally found the carefully folded piece of paper on her prayer mat and flew down the stairs to join the rest of the family in the car.

Once they were strapped in and Mum had begun the drive to the mosque, Yasser and Zahra felt their anticipation grow. Grandfather had told them that everyone's destiny for the whole year was decided on this night and each person could influence that destiny through their du'as.

Yasser's mind was racing. What should he pray for? He looked over to Zahra who was busy re-organising her bag of useful things: a prayer book, tasbih, lots of little papers (probably her notes), a small copy of the Qur'an and a packet of jelly beans, presumably for extra energy. Suddenly Yasser felt under-prepared. His Qur'an and prayer book were with Grandfather, but apart from those, he had taken little else. He patted his pockets and found a small pencil in one and a sad, squashed toffee in the other. Without a second thought, he unwrapped the toffee and popped it into his mouth. Then he asked Zahra for a piece of paper to write down his du'as.

"Things to pray for…" he mouthed the words as he scribbled them across the top.

Yasser tapped the pencil on his chin. There was no point in writing down the obvious things: good health, good grades, the latest Play Station…he didn't need a list to remember to pray for those! Instead, he tried to think of something special, but it was more difficult than he thought it would be. How did Zahra make such long lists?

The car halted abruptly, and Mum switched off the engine. "We're here," she said a little nervously, jangling the keys. Yasser stuffed the paper into his pocket. He would just have to remember whatever he could.

At the main entrance, they stopped before parting ways. Grandfather and Yasser would be in the men's hall, and Mum and Zahra would be with the women.

Mum took Grandfather's hand in her own and kissed the back of his palm. "Please remember us in your du'as," she told him with a tremor in her voice. Grandfather placed his other hand on her head and kissed the top of her forehead.

"May all your du'as be accepted, my daughter. Do not forget me in them," he said to her. Yasser and Zahra looked from one adult to the other; it almost seemed as if Mum and Grandfather were asking each other for a great favour on this night.

"I'll pray for you too," Zahra whispered to Yasser.

Yasser nodded back, not sure what to say. He had a feeling that the du'as of this night were a lot more powerful that he had first imagined.

Once they had removed their shoes and entered the main hall, Yasser stayed close to Grandfather. They sat down in the first empty spots they could see and Grandfather seamlessly joined in with the du'a that was already being recited. Yasser looked up at the translation being projected on the screen at the front of the hall.

> "O Allah, Lord of Ramadhan,
> in which You sent down the Qur'an
>
> and made fasting obligatory on Your servants.
>
> Bless Muhammad and the family of Muhammad
>
> and enable me to go for Hajj to Your sacred House, in this year and in every year.
>
> And forgive me those great sins (that I carry), for surely, none can forgive them except You,
>
> O Beneficent, O All-Knowing."

Yasser recognised this particular du'a because he had recited it every day in Ramadhan, but he had never realised what he was asking for in it. Salawaat was a prayer he recited regularly, and of course, asking for forgiveness every day was a practice of the Holy Prophet, but sandwiched between those two, in the middle of this du'a was a request that he hadn't really thought much about...

*****

Zahra's heart was filled with joy. She had never seen so many people huddled together, their voices creating a low hum as they recited her favourite Ramadhan du'as all together. She squeezed herself next to Mum and began to unpack her bag. She had a long checklist for the night and was on a mission not to let a moment go to waste. She was in the middle of reciting Surah Qadr one hundred times when a tear fell on her lap.

She blinked and realised it was not her own. She looked up and saw Mum immersed in prayer, her tears flowing freely. Zahra looked at the screen to see which du'a had affected Mum so much and read the words:

> "O ALLAH, I ASK YOU TO PLACE IN WHAT YOU DESTINE AND DECREE, FROM THE ORDERS WHICH ARE DEFINITE,
> AND ORDERS WHICH ARE WISE, FROM THE DECREE WHICH IS NOT REVERSED NOR CHANGED,
> WRITE MY NAME AS ONE OF THE PILGRIMS OF YOUR SACRED HOUSE, WHOSE HAJJ IS APPROVED,
> WHOSE EFFORTS ARE APPRECIATED, WHOSE SINS ARE FORGIVEN, AND WHOSE EVIL DEEDS ARE PARDONED...."

Shawwal

Chapter 2

The last few nights of Shahr Ramadhan whizzed by, and Yasser and Zahra had the most fun-filled Eid they could have wished for. Zahra threw her arms around Yasser when she saw the ginormous sweet jar he had bought for her. It was filled with colourful jelly beans with every flavour she could imagine!

Yasser was equally thrilled when he unwrapped the notebook and set of gel pens that Zahra had got for him; it would be a lot more convenient to have his own pens instead of having to borrow hers all the time!

As things slowly returned to their normal routine in the weeks following Eid, Zahra noticed Mum looking more tired than usual. She was taking on extra shifts at work and Zahra missed her on the nights she wasn't back in time to tuck them into bed. She wondered if Mum was hiding something from them, the kind of thing grown-ups worried about on their own without telling their children. She wanted to tell Mum that it was okay to share, that she and Yasser could handle it. They might even be able to help.

The next night Mum was home early, Zahra decided to ask. But first, she made sure that her teeth were clean and she was in her pyjamas having done everything she needed to for bed. She went downstairs to look for Mum and found her at the kitchen table with a cup of steaming tea in one hand and a black and gold leaflet in the other.

Zahra reached out and wrapped her arms around her mother's shoulders from behind. She rested her cheek against her Mum's and sighed. Mum was always so affectionate and comforting. Her skin was warm and soft to touch, and her dark brown hair always smelled of coconuts and vanilla.

"Why are you working so hard, Mum?"

Mum turned around and pulled Zahra into a side hug. She gave her that gentle smile that made Zahra feel like she was the most special person in the world.

"Can I tell you a secret?" she asked in a half whisper.

"YES!" Zahra exclaimed. "Oh please! I love secrets!" In her excitement, she forgot that secrets were usually supposed to be told quietly. She had barely finished speaking when Yasser popped his head into the room, his body still in the hallway.

"DID SOMEONE SAY SECRET?" he asked. "What's going on?" He remained half-in, half-out waiting to decide whether the secret was worth the effort of coming entirely into the kitchen or not.

Mum laughed. Yasser could make Mum laugh like no one else. "Well, I suppose both of you should know..." She held out the leaflet in her hand.

Zahra took it and Yasser came to look over her shoulder. They both recognised the photo on the cover straight away; it was the Holy Kaaba.

"Rayaan Air invites you to join us for Hajj this year," Yasser read the title out loud.

"Well," asked Mum, "what do you think?"

Zahra's eyes widened when she saw the price. So many zeros and that was just for one person! "Is that why you have been working late?" she asked. "To earn some extra money to go for Hajj?"

"Yes!" Mum beamed as she replied. "Hajj is wajib, for every Muslim that can afford it, at least once in their life. This past Shahr Ramadhan I prayed to

Allah to have the chance to go for Hajj. I made the intention even though I knew I didn't quite have enough saved, but alhamdulillah, with all the extra shifts, I now have enough to go and some extra to bring back gifts for you both as well!"

It took a few seconds for her words to sink in, but when they did, the realisation hit the children like a brick wall.

Yasser gulped. "You are going on your own?"

Zahra's face looked like it would crumple any second. "Without us?"

Mum scooped up Yasser and Zahra, one in each arm and hugged them tight. "I'll miss you both so much," she said, squeezing them close, "but this is something I have to do."

Zahra knew how hard Mum worked to make sure that she and Yasser had everything they could possibly want. Looking after them on her own must have been difficult for Mum all these years. This was the first time she was spending money on herself and it was on something that Allah wanted her to do. Zahra knew she had to be strong and support Mum in her decision.

"I'm so happy for you!" She buried her face into Mum's shoulder to hide her tears.

"Me too!" said Yasser. "I didn't know you were so rich!"

When the giggling died down, Mum showed Yasser and Zahra a hadith she had read:

Imam al-Sadiq (as) has said:

'I HAVE NEVER SEEN ANYTHING FASTER AT ATTRACTING WEALTH AND REPELLING POVERTY THAN HABITUAL PILGRIMAGE (HAJJ) TO THIS HOUSE.'

"One of the benefits of Hajj is that it keeps poverty away from you," Mum explained.

"Hang on a minute," Yasser interjected. "You mean that when you spend money in the way of Allah (swt), He gives it back to you?"

"Exactly!" Mum said, nodding.

"That's cool!"

"Isn't it?" Mum patted him on his head. "So, it's

settled then. Tomorrow I will call the travel agent and book my ticket."

It was well past their bedtime, but Mum decided to treat Yasser and Zahra to a mug of milky hot chocolate with gooey marshmallows. They sat around the kitchen table planning Mum's trip and figuring out the things she would need. Mum was so proud of her children and how they always coped in difficult times. She whispered a prayer for their safety and that they too would have the chance to go for Hajj soon. She knew that she would miss them terribly.

dhul qadah

Chapter 3

RING RING! RING RING!

"Has anyone seen my phone?" Mum called from upstairs.

Yasser and Zahra began to hunt, following the buzzing sound. They knew they were close because they could hear the ringtone loudly, but the phone was nowhere to be seen. Yasser fell to his knees and peered under the sofa.

"Aha!" he exclaimed. "Here it is!" he held it out like a pirate finding treasure. "I wonder how it got there..." he was just finishing his sentence when Mum burst into the room.

"Quickly, pass it to me!" Yasser held out the phone. "It could be the travel agent," Mum explained, taking a deep breath before swiping the green button. "Hello.... Alaykum Salaam... yes, this is she...hmm...oh....Alhamdullilah! That's wonderful!" Mum's face broke into a huge smile. "Yes, today is fine...what time? Right now? Of course....Okay see you soon, inshallah."

Mum disconnected the call and held the phone to

her heart. A wide smile remained on her face. Yasser and Zahra stared at her, waiting for an explanation.

"That was the travel agent, Mr Rayaan. He has my ticket and visa ready and he's coming over now to drop them off!"

"That's amazing!" The children hugged Mum. "Congratulations!"

They quickly tidied up the house and when the doorbell rang, they were all ready for Mr. Rayaan. Some of the first things the children noticed about him when they opened the door were Mr Rayaan's wide smile and his pearly white teeth.

"Assalaamu Alaykum! I'm Mr Rayaan of Rayaan Air," he said, his smile never leaving his face as he walked into the living room. He passed Mum a wide envelope with her tickets and travel documents and then told them to feel free to ask any questions.

"Have you ever been for Hajj before?" Zahra wondered.

"Yes! Alhamdullilah, I've been so many times, I've lost count! I try to go every year and help people like your Mum to go as well!"

It sounded like Mr. Rayyan had the best job in the world, Zahra thought to herself.

"In fact, I've been so many times, that now my hair doesn't grow back!" Mr. Rayyan patted his bald head with a laugh.

Zahra didn't understand the joke, but she couldn't help laughing along with him.

"So, it's your job to take people on holiday?" Yasser asked, not quite believing that this qualified as real work.

"Well, Hajj is not a holiday," Mr Rayaan said. "Yes, it's a chance to get away from the business of our daily lives, but our aim is to refocus ourselves on what is truly important, and try to worship Allah (swt) as best we can and improve our faith. It's a physical journey, but most importantly, it's also a journey of the soul." He placed his hand on his chest to emphasize his point.

Yasser and Zahra could see that under his bubbly and fun exterior, Mr Rayyan was sincere in what he believed in. He spoke from his heart and his words touched theirs.

As they drank tea together, the children chatted to Mr Rayaan about his travels. They found out he could speak seven languages and had visited every continent in the world! Soon it was time for him to leave; he had other tickets to deliver, he explained. Before heading out, he gave Mum two papers, one with a checklist of what to pack and another of things to do before her flight.

"If you need anything or have any more questions, don't hesitate to call me or send me a message," he said, giving them one last bright smile before walking to his car.

Mum closed the door and let out a sigh. "I can't believe it's really happening," she said, almost to herself.

Zahra was already reading through the list of things that Mr Rayyan had left. "Unscented soap, white clothes, a money pouch... sounds like we need to go shopping!"

Yasser had the list of things to do before leaving. "Write a will, pay off debts, ask for forgiveness from people you have wronged....Wow! This list makes it sound like you're never coming back..." He looked up at Mum with a worried expression.

Mum smiled and hugged him. "When you go for Hajj, you leave everything in Allah's protection," she said. "And you hope to return as clean as the day you were born, so it's a good idea to look at it as if you are being given a chance to sort out all your affairs and start afresh."

The following weeks flew by with shopping trips, errands, and packing. Yasser and Zahra helped Mum wherever they could, and by the time the date for Mum's travel drew near, the atmosphere in the house was buzzing with energy. The children felt as if they were going on Hajj themselves!

Mrs. Muntazir came to visit and brought so many useful items for Mum: a straw prayer mat, a tasbih with seven beads, and reusable bottle for wudhu. She had thought of all the details. "And don't worry about the children," she said to Mum, putting an arm each around Yasser and Zahra. "Grandfather is here and we'll both keep an eye on them."

dhul hijjah

Chapter 4

Finally, the big day arrived. All their preparation came to good use, and they arrived at the airport in good time without forgetting anything. Yasser and Zahra tried to be brave; they hugged Mum tightly and promised to be good. They smiled till their cheeks hurt while waving at Mum until they couldn't see her anymore, but in the car on the way home, they were unusually silent. When Grandfather looked in the rear-view mirror, Zahra was looking down at her hands and letting out tiny, whispery sniffs and Yasser was staring out the window, his lip wobbling a little. The next few weeks were going to be tough for them, he thought.

"Well kids, Mum is off on her journey of a lifetime," he said to them cheerily. "We'll need to make sure that we have some adventures of our own while she's away!"

They half-smiled back at him, but their expressions didn't brighten up. Grandfather sighed inwardly. He would have to come up with an idea that would take them on their best adventure yet.

When they arrived home, the house seemed eerily quiet and empty. How could one person make such a difference? Zahra wondered to herself. But then she realised, it wasn't just any one person who was missing, it was Mum. Her mind immediately went to all the children in the world who no longer had their mothers with them and she sent up a prayer to Allah to give them strength and patience, just as Mum always reminded them to every night.

Grandfather had already made his way to the kitchen to prepare some lunch. Mum had left some freshly baked falafels in the oven so all he had to do was spread creamy hummus on some flat bread wraps, pile in crunchy lettuce and cucumbers before carefully placing the still-warm falafels on top. He followed with more sauce, wrapped each roll up tightly and cut each one in half. Impressed with his own work, he called out to Yasser and Zahra. The sight and scent of the food cheered them up a little and they all sat down to eat together.

"I was hungrier than I thought!" Zahra exhaled.

"Me too!" Yasser added. "That was delicious Grandfather."

After they had cleared up the table and put away the dishes, Yasser tugged at Grandfather's sleeve. "Grandfather, I've been thinking. Why has Allah made Hajj wajib for every person at least once in their lifetime?"

"Fantastic question!" Grandfather replied with energy. "Come with me and let's find out!" He gestured to the children to follow him to the prayer room. There, he sat in his favourite chair and pulled out a copy of the Holy Qur'an. He kissed the book, touched it to his forehead and then with a soft "Bismillah", opened it to show the children the chapter called Surah Hajj.

"Wow!" said Zahra. "A whole surah named after Hajj? It must be a really important journey."

Grandfather nodded. He let his fingers glide over the page as if just touching the verses brought him peace, until he finally said, "Look here at verses 27 and 28."

Yasser peered over Grandfather's shoulder and read out the English translation.

"CALL ALL PEOPLE TO THE HAJJ. THEY WILL COME TO YOU ON FOOT AND ON EVERY LEAN CAMEL FROM EVERY DISTANT PATH, SO THEY MAY OBTAIN THE BENEFITS IN STORE FOR THEM..."

As she listened to Yasser read, a thousand questions began to race through Zahra's mind. *Who was making the call? It said all people... wasn't Hajj just for Muslims? What kinds of benefits was the verse talking about? And what about people who couldn't go for Hajj? Did they get any benefits?*

Grandfather watched her face. He could tell when she had her thinking cap on and he smiled, knowing the questions would start bubbling out of her soon.

Yasser was more practical and it was the image of people walking and coming on all different vehicles to Hajj that caught his attention. He repeated the phrase: "They will come to you on foot and on every lean camel…"

THUD!

Yasser jumped with a gasp and Zahra let out a little yelp. What was that sound? They both turned to where the sudden noise had come from and saw that Grandfather's magical green rug was on the ground. It was almost as if it had jumped from the shelf where it was so neatly kept and unfurled itself. On closer inspection, the rug seemed to be quivering slightly, as if it was waiting impatiently for something.

"Well, it's not a camel, but…" Yasser mused. "Grandfather, do you think that we could go?"

"Oh, please Grandfather," Zahra pleaded. "I have so many questions that I need to find the answers to!"

Grandfather chuckled. "In that case," he said,

"LET ME TELL YOU A STORY…"

They all climbed onto the rug and with a familiar, thrilling **WHOOOOOOSSSSHHH**, they were off!

Chapter 5

Yasser, Zahra, and Grandfather held on tight to the rug as it soared through the air, the wind whistling past their ears. There was a flash of light and when it faded, the children looked down to see tall minarets of a beautiful mosque below them. Millions of people of all colours, shapes and sizes were pouring out of the mosque, reciting what seemed to be praises of Allah in unison.

"Let's go closer!" Yasser said, hoping to be able to hear what the people were saying more clearly. The rug hummed in response and lowered itself until the children could gain a better view of the scene below.

"We have arrived at the **MIQAT**." Grandfather announced, sounding like a pilot. "It is where pilgrims go to make their intention and put on their ihram, the special white clothes, to perform Hajj and Umrah."

"It's so difficult to spot Mum in this crowd," Zahra said, feeling like there was a small Mum-shaped hole in her heart. "Everyone looks the same!"

"That's the point, Zahra!" Yasser said. He whacked his sister on the arm and pointed at the masses. "Now you can't tell who is rich, who is poor, or where a person is from…"

"Or which one is Mum!" Zahra said, rubbing the spot he had smacked. "That hurt by the way."

"Sorry," Yasser said, grinning. "I was trying to make a point."

"Ahem…" Grandfather cleared his throat to get their attention. "Yasser, you're absolutely right.

Allah (swt) is reminding us not look at the things we usually use to tell the difference between each other. In the Qur'an, Allah (swt) says that the best of people is the one who has the most taqwa. Pilgrims understand that Allah cares about what is on the inside, not the clothes and jewellery we wear. That's why when they exchange their normal clothes for ihram, the pilgrims think of it as taking off the clothes of sin and putting on the clothes of obedience to Allah (swt)."

Yasser beamed and puffed his chest out. It had been a long time since he had made a point before Zahra.

"Who would have thought there would be special reasons just for the clothes you wear!" Zahra said. "What else is special about ihram?"

"Well, it's not just the clothes you wear, it's your whole state. It's similar to when you begin your salaat and say Takbiratul Ihram, the first Allahu Akbar. At that time your whole self is directed to Allah and some of things you can usually do become haram for you while you are praying."

"So when a person puts on their ihram, their whole self is directed to Allah..." Zahra said, trying to compare what Grandfather had said to what they were seeing. "Wait...what do you mean by things become haram when we are praying?" she asked, confused.

"Well, you can't eat or drink," Grandfather explained, "or laugh or turn away from the qiblah... and those are just a few examples. Even when you fast, eating and drinking, which is usually allowed during the day, becomes haram. In the same way, when you are in the state of ihram for Hajj or umrah, twenty-five things become haram."

"TWENTY-FIVE EXTRA THINGS?" Yasser exclaimed. **"THAT'S LOADS!"**

"You'd have to be always watching yourself to make sure you didn't do any of those things!" Zahra added.

"Exactly! Being constantly aware of yourself and your actions is very important in life and more so during pilgrimage. Some of the things that are forbidden are to do with the body, like not wearing perfume and not looking in the mirror, or to do with keeping peace, so you are not allowed to hunt or carry weapons or even kill a single bug, or to control your behaviour so you cannot lie or quarrel with each other when in ihram."

Yasser remembered he had one of his new gel pens in his pocket. He quickly made a wobbly list of some of the things that pilgrims were forbidden from doing in the state of ihram. Hajj was about focusing on Allah (swt) and it seemed that He had thought of every detail to stop people from getting distracted from that goal. *It's like we must pause the body for a while, so that the heart can wake up*, he thought to himself.

- No perfume
- Don't look in the mirror
- No sewn clothes for men
- No hunting
- No cutting nails or hair

They continued to float gently above the scene below, where it looked like a river of overflowing milk was pouring out of the mosque as group upon group of white clad pilgrims flowed down the streets reciting praises to Allah in Arabic.

"What are they reciting?" Yasser asked, remembering why he had asked for the rug to bring them closer to the crowds.

"That is the Talbiyyah." Grandfather replied. He recited the words along with the crowd, joining them in perfect time.

لَبَّيْكَ ٱللَّهُمَّ لَبَّيْكَ

Here I am [at Your service] O Allah, here I am.

لَبَّيْكَ لَا شَرِيكَ لَكَ لَبَّيْكَ

Here I am [at Your service].

You have no partners (other gods), here I am.

إِنَّ ٱلْحَمْدَ وَ ٱلنِّعْمَةَ لَكَ وَ ٱلْمُلْكَ

To You alone is all praise and all excellence,

and to You is all sovereignty.

لَا شَرِيكَ لَكَ لَبَّيْكَ

There is no partner to You. Here I am.

Hearing the people praising Allah and glorifying Him with beautiful chants of "Labbayk", something unlocked in Yasser's heart, his tongue became free, and he joined in with the crowd, following the words they were reciting.

Zahra listened to each phrase keenly. It was as if the people were responding to a question they had been asked. Suddenly, she remembered the verse that had brought them here. "They are replying to the call mentioned in the Qur'an!"

"Well remembered, Zahra!" Grandfather beamed, pleased that his granddaughter had been paying attention. "I suppose you'd like to know who made that call?"

"Yes! Please!" Zahra exclaimed. She looked ready to explode with curiosity.

"In that case, I think there is someone we need to meet!" Grandfather tugged at one corner of the rug; it responded, circling the crowd one more time and zooming into the air and through another tunnel of light.

Chapter 6

When the trio came out through the light again, the rug made a dusty landing in the middle of a bustling marketplace. Yasser and Zahra looked at the mud buildings and the raw cotton clothes that the people were wearing and immediately realised that they were no longer in the present. They had travelled back in time! Zahra recalled their past adventures and was sure that wherever they were was long before the time of Prophet Muhammad or any of the Imams. Yasser thought it might be even before the time of Prophet Isa.

Just as they were about to ask Grandfather where they were, an argument broke out between a man and a shopkeeper at a stall nearby.

"I PAID YOU FIFTY COINS FOR THIS!" the man was shouting, shaking a small stone statue in his left hand. "That was all the money I had!"

"It is worth **MUCH MORE!**" the shopkeeper responded, red-faced.

"You said it would bring me luck and heal my son. I have prayed day and night and offered my best sacrifice, but my son is getting sicker by the day! He has no strength to walk or even open his eyes!" The furious man was almost in tears.

"You will have to be patient," the shopkeeper shrugged casually. "The gods cannot be rushed. These things take time."

A crowd had now gathered around the two men. The buyer's fists were clenched and he looked as if he was going to punch the shopkeeper. Just then a young man broke from the crowd and came to stand between the shopkeeper and the desperate man.

"Why do you insist on worshipping these gods of wood and stone?" he asked in a gentle tone. "They cannot benefit you or harm you..."

"YOU DON'T KNOW WHAT YOU ARE TALKING ABOUT!" the shopkeeper roared. "We have worshipped these gods for generations." He waved his hand towards the array of statues in his shop. "Our fathers and their fathers have all done the same thing; why should we do any different?"

The young man turned to the crowd and challenged the people there. "Have you really thought about what you are worshipping? And your ancestors too! They are all enemies to me – except for the Lord of the worlds."

The marketplace fell silent. The hustle and bustle became quiet as vendors and shoppers alike froze. All eyes were on this young man who had dared to question the way they had always done things.

Yasser thought the man was very brave. He looked closer at him and realised from his delicate features and soft beard that he was a lot younger than Yasser had originally thought. He wasn't even a grown man, just a youth! Yet his words were filled with reason and calm confidence.

"Who is he?" Zahra asked in a whisper. "He must be someone very special..." Before Zahra could finish her sentence, the young man spoke again. He said to the people that he had only told them what not to worship, now he wanted to describe his God to them.

"He is the One who created me. He alone guides me. He is the One who provides me with food and drink..." He then turned to the man who had been arguing with the shopkeeper and gently placed his hand on the man's shoulder, looking into his eyes, and speaking directly to his soul. "He alone heals me when I am sick. He is the One who will cause me to die and bring me back to life. And He alone is the One that I hope will forgive my flaws on Judgement Day."

For a few seconds, the desperate man looked like he was thinking seriously about what he had just heard. He did not get the chance to speak though because the shopkeeper stepped forward, the veins on his forehead standing out in red, angry lines.

"Get away from us, you crazy boy!" He yelled, waving the people away. As the crowd dispersed, the young man's face fell in disappointment. The shopkeeper wasn't done with him though. He came closer and spoke through clenched teeth in a voice that was just loud enough for the time travellers to hear. "If you were not Azar's nephew, I would have told them to kill you! Think twice before you speak against our gods again, Ibrahim!"

Yasser gasped. "This is Prophet Ibrahim?" He looked up at Grandfather, who nodded in confirmation.

"This is Babylonia, and yes Yasser, that is Prophet Ibrahim (as)!"

"I just knew he was a prophet!" Zahra exclaimed. "I love the way he described Allah with so much love, as if Allah is his best friend!"

"Well, what are we doing just standing here?" Yasser said. "We need to follow him!"

Chapter 7

Prophet Ibrahim walked away from the busy marketplace. Yasser, Zahra and Grandfather followed closely on the rug, bobbing gently behind him like a second shadow. Prophet Ibrahim walked humbly, his head low, deeply lost in thought.

Perhaps he is talking to Allah and wondering why the people will not listen to him, Zahra thought. *Or perhaps, Allah is whispering in his heart and telling him about the wonders of the heavens and the earth.* She shivered at the idea of having a personal conversation with her Creator, what an amazing experience that would be!

The shadows became longer and the sky grew darker, yet Prophet Ibrahim continued on his solitary trek until he was past the city walls and far into the quiet desert beyond it. As night fell completely, it became harder to see where they were going until they spotted a faint gleam in the distance.

"It's a fire," Yasser said, pointing towards the flickering light. "And there are people there too!"

"It looks like Prophet Ibrahim is heading towards them," Zahra said.

As they got closer, they saw Prophet Ibrahim join the group. Those gathered were looking up at the starry night and chanting.

"What are they saying?" Zahra asked, her voice in a hushed whisper even though no one could hear her.

"They are praying to the **STARS**," Grandfather replied, pointing up at the glittering night sky. The children had never seen so many stars before. Without any electricity or lights to outshine them, the stars sparkled like scattered jewels. There were too many to see, let alone count.

"How come Prophet Ibrahim is with them?" Yasser asked, a little confused. "Why doesn't he stop them like he did the people in the marketplace."

It was true, Prophet Ibrahim was behaving differently. He was talking to the group of star worshippers, and watching carefully as they showed him their practices. Zahra could see that the group had taken an immediate liking to Prophet Ibrahim because of his polite nature and humble manner. They welcomed him into their group and talked to him like he was an old friend. However, as night progressed and the full moon rose, some of the stars began to fade. Prophet Ibrahim looked up with remorse and said aloud to the group. "I do not love things that set." He got up, took their leave and walked away.

The group seemed bewildered, as if they had never noticed that the beautiful celestial stars were not permanent. They began talking amongst themselves, discussing what Prophet Ibrahim had just said.

Yasser was amazed. "I love how Prophet Ibrahim showed them the reality of the situation and then let them figure stuff out for themselves. He's teaching them not to follow other people blindly and to think about things."

Zahra nodded. "I thought that we were not allowed to question things when they don't make sense to us. Sometimes we are taught things and just told to accept. That makes us no different from the people that Prophet Ibrahim is preaching to, right Grandfather?"

Grandfather had always tried to encourage his grandchildren to ask questions, but he knew it was now time to explain more. "True knowledge is not about memorising facts and storing information. Allah (swt) encourages us to observe and then to think and reflect so we can understand our beliefs and allow them to impact our lives. However, there are boundaries, and we need to remember that once we have submitted to Allah (swt), we cannot question His Command," Grandfather looked from Yasser to Zahra. "Let's continue to follow Prophet Ibrahim and you'll soon get to see that Prophet Ibrahim understood exactly when to question and when to submit."

They stayed with Prophet Ibrahim until he reached a second group of people who were worshipping the **MOON**. Again, he sat with them and asked them about their faith, just as he had with the first group. However, as dawn approached and the moon set, Prophet Ibrahim shook his head and stood up to leave. He looked up at the brightening heavens and said, "If my Lord does not guide me, I will surely be of those who are astray." Once again, the group he left behind were amazed by his behaviour and began to wonder about their own.

As the day progressed and the sun rose in the cloudless, blue sky, Prophet Ibrahim started to make his way back to the city. He stopped at an oasis to refresh himself and drink some water. Zahra watched him carefully. Everything he did was measured. He paused before every action, as if thinking about it before performing it. There was an inner calmness that seemed to radiate from him even in the simplest of things. She wished she had the same kind of peace, it seemed like such a wonderful thing to have.

As the city walls came into view in the distance, Prophet Ibrahim came across a third group – this time it was a group who were worshipping the **SUN**. He joined with them once again. Yasser and Zahra wondered how anyone could worship the sun.

"The sun is a source of light and heat for all of us," Grandfather explained. "In our time, we understand the science behind its existence and the energy it provides for us. However, in the ancient times, all people knew was that the sun drove away the darkness of the night. They could see how its warmth helped them and how plants and crops grew when it shone. They even saw the effects of too much sunlight and how it could destroy the same plants if it got too hot. These people confused the power of the sun and the One Who created the sun."

"The power of the sun..." Yasser wondered. "Hmm...there are so many times when we think we have power, or that something happened because we made it happen...does that mean that we worship ourselves?" he chuckled. He said it as a bit of a joke, but Grandfather seemed to take his comment seriously.

"Yes, Yasser, you're absolutely right," Grandfather said, giving him a thoughtful look.

"I am?" Yasser was surprised. That was the kind of thing Grandfather usually told Zahra. Maybe he was growing up and becoming more like her. He wasn't sure he was ready to grow up, that would mean being more... *responsible*. He shook his head, brushing the thought away.

"Believing that we are the ones who make anything happen is called arrogance. We'll soon see a great example of arrogance..."

While Yasser was talking to Grandfather, Zahra was focused on the way Prophet Ibrahim looked at the world. "Grandfather?" she asked. "Prophet Ibrahim keeps rejecting all these gods that the people are worshipping because he says they are temporary and cannot help. He seems to want people to figure out what God is not supposed to be. But...how can we know what Allah is really like?"

Grandfather smiled widely. This was the question he had really been hoping the children would ask. This was the lesson that Prophet Ibrahim had been trying to teach all his life!

"Zahra, my dearest, the answer to your question is inside you, it is inside each and every one of us. Allah is the greatest possible being and the most worthy of worship! If you want to know what He is like, you simply need to imagine what kind of being you would dedicate your whole life to, what would He need to be like for you to worship Him? What are the best qualities you can think of?"

"Well..." Zahra started to think. "He would have to be kind and loving. He would have to be able to hear me when I call Him and see everything all the time so that He can be fair, He would have to know everything..."

"And He would have to be powerful too!" said Yasser, jumping into the discussion. "There's no point worshipping a god who can't help you!"

Grandfather nodded encouragingly. "That's a great start. Now look around you, ask yourself just as Prophet Ibrahim did, can you worship something that cannot help you or harm you? Can you worship something that disappears?"

Zahra looked back at Prophet Ibrahim, who was still talking to the sun worshippers. She remembered the way he had described Allah in the marketplace.

He is the One who created me...that was Power... He alone guides me...that was Knowledge. He is the One who provides me with food and drink... Kindness...He alone heals me when I am sick... Loving...He alone is the One that I hope will forgive my flaws on Judgement Day... Power and Kindness together!

"Oh Allah, you are exactly as I want you to be." A hot, happy tear slid down Zahra's cheek as she made a prayer deep from her heart Allah. "Please, please, make me the way You want me to be..."

Chapter 8

As the sun began to set over the golden sand dunes, Prophet Ibrahim left the last group of worshippers. He turned his back to the setting sun and proclaimed that he worshipped One God alone. "I have turned my face towards the One Who has originated the heavens and the earth—being upright—and I am not one of the polytheists."

"What's a **POLYTHEIST**?" Yasser asked.

"It is someone who believes in more than one god," Grandfather replied. "And a monotheist is someone who worships only one god."

"I think if there was more than one god, they would just end up fighting with each other," Yasser said. "One might want it to be night and the other day, or one would want it to rain and the other for it be dry...it would be chaos!"

"And they would be limited in their power too," said Zahra. "Because they would have to share being god!"

"Precisely. That's why we believe in an unlimited God," Grandfather said. "And why Prophet Ibrahim is called the Father of Monotheism."

"Which is the opposite of polytheism I assume?" Zahra asked, half guessing.

"Exactly! Monotheism is worshipping One God!" Grandfather smiled.

Yasser, Zahra and Grandfather followed Prophet Ibrahim back into the city and through its streets until they stopped outside a towering mansion with beautifully carved pillars and gigantic elaborate statues flanking both sides of its huge entrance.

"This can't be where Prophet Ibrahim lives!" Yasser exclaimed in shock. "He's a prophet and all prophets lived simple lives!"

"Not all," Grandfather clarified. "Some of them had a lot of wealth, they just never got attached to it or distracted by it. In Prophet Ibrahim's case, this is the house of his uncle, Azar, who brought him up. His uncle was a famous maker and seller of idols."

Yasser and Zahra tried to digest this double whammy. Prophet Ibrahim was surrounded not only by wealth, but also by a stubborn idol worshipper! How had he stayed so firm in his belief and always acted with humility?

The news of what had happened in the marketplace had travelled fast it seemed. Azar was waiting at the door for his nephew's return, his face bright red with anger.

"What do you think you are doing?" Azar bellowed as soon as he caught sight of Prophet Ibrahim. "Why did you stir up trouble in the marketplace?" He did not let Prophet Ibrahim reply. "Why will you not pray to these idols?" He demanded, gesturing to the statues on either side of them. "I am the best idol maker in the city and I have made these with my own hands!"

Prophet Ibrahim came closer and looked deeply into Azar's eyes. He gently took Azar's hands before asking, "My dear father, who made these two hands of yours?"

Azar snatched his hands back and turned away in a rage. Prophet Ibrahim did not give up. He approached him again and placed a hand on Azar's shoulder. "O my dear father, why do you insist on worshipping what can neither hear nor see, nor benefit you at all?"

Azar folded his arms and furrowed his eyebrows. Prophet Ibrahim kept trying to get through to him,

"O my dear father! I have certainly received some knowledge which you have not received, so follow me and I will guide you to the Straight Path. O my dear father! Do not worship Shaitan. Surely Shaitan is ever rebellious against the Most Compassionate."

At this, Azar began to walk away. Prophet Ibrahim tried to catch up with him. It seemed that he cared deeply about his uncle and hated seeing him worship idols instead of the one true God. He wanted to make sure he had tried every argument to convince his uncle. He pleaded once again, "Dear father! I truly fear that you will be touched by a torment from the Most Compassionate and become Shaitan's companion in Hell."

Azar turned around and shot a piercing stare his nephew. When Prophet Ibrahim's gentle expression did not change, his eyes narrowed in frustration. He grabbed Prophet Ibrahim's shirt in clenched fists and spat in his face. **"HOW DARE YOU REJECT MY IDOLS, O IBRAHIM! IF YOU DON'T STOP THIS BEHAVIOUR, I WILL CERTAINLY STONE YOU TO DEATH!"**

Azar let go of the shirt and threw his nephew to the floor. "Be gone from me for a long time!"

Prophet Ibrahim sat up and called out after his uncle. "Peace be upon you! I will pray to my Lord for your forgiveness. He has truly been Most Gracious to me."

Yasser and Zahra looked at each other in shock.

"How could Prophet Ibrahim be so loving and polite to his uncle after everything he just did?" Yasser asked. "If it was me, I would have punched him back! Or at least told Azar to get lost!"

"And why did Prophet Ibrahim keep calling him dear father? I thought he was his uncle?" Zahra added.

"Prophet Ibrahim is called **HALEEM**, which means tender-hearted," said Grandfather. "He truly cared about all people and wanted them to be safe from ignorance and hellfire. Azar had looked after Prophet Ibrahim when he was a child, that is why he called him 'father'."

Zahra thought about all the times she had fought with Yasser. She would sulk, he would stomp around, and they would both shout as if they hated each other. It was usually over something so simple, like who got to hold the TV remote or who ate the last chocolate chip cookie. Prophet Ibrahim was so different. He was firm in his beliefs, but also so kind and gentle. How much love did it take to wish peace on an evil uncle like Azar!

"I am going to try to be more like Prophet Ibrahim," Zahra said determinedly to herself.

Chapter 9

Yasser, Zahra and Grandfather spent the evening huddled on the rug, talking about Prophet Ibrahim's amazing character. They talked about the incredible combination of qualities that Prophet Ibrahim had. Yasser loved Prophet Ibrahim's curiosity about the world and how he questioned things so that his faith in one God grew stronger and stronger. Zahra admired the fact that Prophet Ibrahim always relied on God to guide him, that his heart was soft and tender, and he genuinely cared about people.

"All those things in one person!" said Yasser. "That's super awesome."

"Prophet Ibrahim is our role model," said Grandfather. "He is pretty amazing. In the Qur'an, he is referred to as a nation by himself."

Zahra was duly impressed. "Does the Qur'an say anything else about Prophet Ibrahim?"

Grandfather's eyes widened. "Yasser, Zahra, my dears, **PROPHET IBRAHIM IS THE HERO OF THE QUR'AN! TWO HUNDRED AND FORTY-FIVE VERSES OF THE QUR'AN REFER TO HIM!**"

"Subhanallah! Allah must love Prophet Ibrahim so much!"

"He does," agreed Grandfather. "That's why He gave Prophet Ibrahim the title of **KHALILALLAH**."

"What does that mean?" Yasser asked.

"Khalil Allah means Friend of Allah," Grandfather said.

Yasser and Zahra looked at each other; this was no ordinary man they were witnessing. They continued talking about what it meant to be Allah's friend and Grandfather explained that it was not an easy title to earn; Prophet Ibrahim had needed to prove himself before being given such a high status.

The children were about to ask what he had done to prove himself when they got distracted by the activity around them. Merchants had begun to hang colourful banners on their shops and the city priests were opening the huge temple doors. Yasser and Zahra rushed over to have a closer look.

"It looks like they are preparing for a celebration!" Yasser said.

"You're right!" agreed Zahra. "Look over there! There's a huge crowd leaving the city." She pointed in the distance.

"It looks so cool!" said Yasser. "Please can we join them?"

Grandfather looked at the enthusiastic children and nodded. There was a lesson to be learned even in this. The glitter and excitement of the festival had captured their attention. The colourful flags and beating drums were attractive, but he was surprised they hadn't asked what the celebration was about. They just wanted to join in the fun. *How many times do we do this in our daily lives?* He wondered to himself. *Celebrating festivals and taking part in festivities without question, simply because we want to be part of the crowd.*

They walked slowly behind the crowd that was leaving the city. They watched as the idol worshippers danced, prayed, and played music, enjoying the festival together. The little children were dressed in their finest clothes, the women had worn jewellery that sparkled in the sun and the men led the front of the crowd. The numbers swelled as they continued for a distance outside of the city and then stopped to have a feast. It was some time before Zahra looked around and had a sudden realisation.

"It looks like everyone from the city is here!" She said, trying to shout over the loud noises of merriment. "Where is Prophet Ibrahim?"

"I can't see him!" Yasser shouted back. "In fact, I have not seen him all day..."

Zahra's smile disappeared and she suddenly felt as if she couldn't stay at the festival for a second longer. She had to get out. She looked to Grandfather who had been extremely quiet and asked if they could leave. He nodded in relief.

"Yasser, let's go," she said, tugging his shirt sleeve. Yasser followed willingly, he wanted to find out what had happened to Prophet Ibrahim too.

They rushed back to the city to find it completed deserted. They searched the marketplace and even went back to Azar's house, but they could not find Prophet Ibrahim. As they completed a full circle and returned to the marketplace, they saw the townspeople starting to filter back from the festival. The men, women walked back slowly in small groups, carrying or dragging along their tired children. The priests brought up the rear, returning to their temple to close the doors for the day.

As they watched the crowds, hoping for a glimpse of Prophet Ibrahim somewhere, Yasser and Zahra heard a commotion rise up from the temple arena. The children and Grandfather quickly ran along the narrow streets to see what was going on. They pushed through the crowd and stopped at the temple courtyard. Spread out in front of them were piles of broken pieces of wood and crumbled clay. In the middle of the rubble was one large idol with an axe hanging at an awkward angle around its neck.

The head priest was fuming. "Who dared do this to our gods?" he asked the growing crowd. "Where is the evildoer who committed this crime?"

A man from the crowd shouted out: "I know a young man called Ibrahim who speaks badly of our gods! It must be him!"

Yasser gasped; he grabbed Zahra's hand. "It's the shopkeeper that Prophet Ibrahim had an argument with! He's trying to get him in trouble!"

"AZAR!" The head priest screamed. "Bring Ibrahim here at once! The people can witness his trial!"

Chapter 10

Yasser and Zahra grabbed on to Grandfather's hands as they watched Azar scramble away to fetch his nephew.

"I wish we had not left the city today," Zahra said, squeezing Grandfather's fingers. "Oh, I wish we had stayed behind!"

Yasser was silent, but as he watched the crowd around the temple grow larger and the mood get more and more hostile, he felt his chest tighten and his heart begin to beat faster. These people were neither gentle nor friendly. What would they do to Prophet Ibrahim?

After what seemed like hours, but was probably just minutes, Azar returned, pulling his nephew by the arm. The crowd parted and let the two men through, closing tightly behind them as soon as they passed. Azar pushed Prophet Ibrahim in front of the high priest and then stepped back, as if to distance himself from whatever was going to happen next.

The head priest glared at the young man but Prophet Ibrahim was not intimidated and looked back at him calmly. "Was it you who did this to our gods, Ibrahim?" he yelled.

Prophet Ibrahim stood tall. He looked around casually at the rubble with a slightly curious expression on his face. The silence was almost deafening as everyone waited for him to respond. When he finally spoke, Prophet Ibrahim simply said: "No." He paused for a moment and then, with a small smile, pointed to the big idol. "This one—the biggest of them—did it. So, ask them, if they can talk."

Zahra couldn't believe her ears. "Is he blaming the big statue for breaking all the others?"

Yasser started to giggle. "Oh, you're too clever, Prophet Ibrahim! The idol can't even hold the axe, let alone use it!" He couldn't stop laughing with relief. Everyone was looking at the giant idol with the axe hung around it's neck; surely they would be able to see how ridiculous the situation was.

Murmurs began to spread through the crowd. The people seemed bewildered at Prophet Ibrahim's simple challenge. They knew that their gods could not speak or hear or act. There was no way that the big statue could have done anything.

One person spoke out, "You already know that these idols cannot talk!"

Prophet Ibrahim jumped at the chance to make them think. "Do you then worship—instead of Allah—what can neither benefit nor harm you in any way?" The crowd fell silent once again. When no one responded, he continued, "Shame on you and whatever you worship instead of Allah! Don't you have any sense?"

People were starting to look at each other in confusion. They could understand that Prophet Ibrahim had asked them to consider something very important. It was something they had blindly followed without question and now they were beginning to doubt their beliefs. The head priest could see that he was losing control over the crowd. Prophet Ibrahim had made their gods look like fools! He needed to be silenced before people started to think about what he was saying!

"Why don't they just listen to Prophet Ibrahim?" Yasser asked. "He's making perfect sense. How can you worship stone idols that you have made yourself? It should be a simple thing to understand!"

"Sometimes, when people are stubborn in their ignorance and insist that they are right, they become easy to control. Pride and stubbornness are two tools that Shaitan uses to misguide us," Grandfather said. "Prophet Ibrahim was encouraging people to start thinking for themselves, and this scared those in power very much."

Although there was no evidence to prove that Prophet Ibrahim had done anything wrong, it was obvious that he was responsible for breaking the idols. The high priest consulted with the other officials and after a few short minutes they turned to Prophet Ibrahim with a verdict.

"We have decided that there is only one way to avenge our gods!" the head priest announced. "Ibrahim must burn!"

"BURN HIM! BURN HIM! BURN HIM!" the priest starting to chant and soon the entire crowd was shouting at the top of their voices. The words filled the air and thundered across the city.

Zahra looked at Yasser and Grandfather in dismay. "Are they really going to kill Prophet Ibrahim for this?" she asked in disbelief, as they watched the priests drag Prophet Ibrahim away.

Yasser really hoped that the answer was no, but he could see how violently angry the crowd was. It was scary just watching the hard lines of their faces, almost as if they had become monsters instead of humans.

"Look!" Yasser said, "They're already collecting firewood!"

A circle had been cleared in the temple courtyard and people were already gathering anything they could find that would burn. The pyre grew until it was heads and shoulders higher than Grandfather, who was quite tall.

"Surely they don't need to make such a big fire," Zahra said in a small voice.

"You're right," Grandfather replied, "but they want to make an example of Prophet Ibrahim. The priests are hoping that by doing this, they will scare anyone else who dares to even think about saying or doing anything against their idols."

Suddenly, drumbeats began to echo through the town. Zahra could feel the stones beneath her feet tremble. Foot soldiers with tall sharp spears appeared in a marching procession, behind them came a golden chariot pulled by two magnificent stallions, followed by more soldiers. When the party reached the giant pile of firewood, the drumbeats stopped abruptly. A hush fell over the crowd who were staring at the chariot in awe.

"Lower your heads for the King!" a booming voice commanded and the crowd obeyed immediately. Azar was almost doubling over in their eagerness to show his respect.

At first, Yasser and Zahra could only see a deep purple, crushed-velvet cloak appear from the chariot. When the cloak descended, a soldier stepped forward to take it off and the man who emerged from its folds was small and shrew-like. As he turned to face the crowd, Yasser and Zahra got a good glimpse of him. He wore a wide golden collar around his neck that held his chin up and made him appear taller than his height. His long, sharp, pointy nose tilted upward which made him look even more arrogant every time he looked down on the people with a smirk.

"That is King Namrood," Grandfather said. "He says that he is the greatest god and that is why he has come to witness Prophet Ibrahim's execution."

King Namrood surveyed the situation and his nostrils flared with anger at the sight of the broken idols. He ordered for even more firewood to be brought and both civilians and soldiers alike rushed to do as he commanded. Another group of the royal guards began setting the pyre alight. Soon, a colossal inferno had roared to life. Flames, like ravenous serpents, coiled and leaped in hues of orange, crimson, and gold. The aroma of burning wood and singed earth mingled in the air.

The crowd was pushed by back the heat and smoke.

"Where is Prophet Ibrahim?" Yasser asked between coughs. He held up his sleeve to cover his nose and mouth. It was getting hard to breath.

Zahra's looked around and spotted him tied to a pole to one side. There was a tranquil look on his face as he looked up to the skies, his mouth moving in silent whispers. *He must be talking to his Friend*, Zahra thought, *to Allah*. She had seen this look before on the plains of Karbala. She also remembered the devastation that occurred there and prayed for Prophet Ibrahim's safety.

"Let's go closer," Yasser suggested.

As they approached the pole where he was tied up, they could hear what Prophet Ibrahim was saying: "Allah is sufficient for us, and He is the best supporter." The words fell from his lips softly, again and again. "*Hasbunallah, wa ni'mal wakeel.*"

"Prophet Ibrahim has such strong trust and faith that Allah will always look after him," Yasser whispered in awe.

"I told you both that Prophet Ibrahim was the Father of Monotheism," Grandfather reminded him. "This is what we call true **TAWHEED**."

Yasser and Zahra knew about tawheed. They had learned about it at Islamic school and understood the phrase 'la ilaha illa Allah,' to mean that 'there is no god but Allah.' They also knew that Surah Ikhlas was also called Surah Tawheed and that belief in one God is at the centre of Islam.

However, the tawheed Prophet Ibrahim was showing them was not just something he had read about in a book, it was something he applied to every experience and every day. He had rejected worshipping the stars, moon and sun as gods, and he had refused to worship the idols that his community was devoted to. Instead, he had chosen to worship the One God, because that is what he knew to be true in his mind and heart.

So far, they had seen Prophet Ibrahim living for tawheed and now they were witnessing how he was willing to die for it as well. He knew that Allah is watching him, and that He is in charge of everything, all the time and that was all that mattered to him. Whatever happened was the Will of Allah and he did not question it and he was happy to submit to it.

Chapter 11

"What's happening?" Yasser asked, standing on his tip toes. The soldiers had untied Prophet Ibrahim and dragged him towards the front of the fire ten minutes ago, but nothing had happened yet. The blaze was growing hotter, and the crowd was getting restless. Cries of "Throw him in already!" and "Burn Ibrahim!" rose from the crowd. Yasser and Zahra tried to peer through the bodies to spot anything. There seemed to be a commotion amongst the soldiers.

"The fire is too big," said Grandfather who could see above the heads of the people. "They don't know how to throw Prophet Ibrahim into the fire!"

"Maybe this is how Allah (swt) will save him!" Zahra cried happily.

Her hopes were dashed in a few minutes when she saw the commander send off a regiment of soldiers who soon reappeared pushing a contraption that looked like a large spade with a long arm.

"Is that a...catapult?" she asked, her heart sinking at the implication.

The soldiers positioned the catapult at a safe distance and then placed Prophet Ibrahim in its curved hand.

"I can't look!" Yasser said covering his eyes. Zahra put her arms around him to try to comfort him and buried her face in his shoulder. She couldn't believe this was happening.

They heard King Namrood issue the order to release the catapult and then the soft *shhhhh* of the rope. Zahra threw a quick glance upwards and saw Prophet Ibrahim's body flying towards the top of the fire. She drew in a sharp breath and hugged Yasser, who was sobbing, tighter.

The gathering burst into cheers as the celebrations broke out and it seemed that they were the only ones mourning. Once the people had their fill of chanting and clapping, the people began to disperse. There seemed nothing else to do now except wait for the fire to die out.

It was then, as the crowds began to thin, that Zahra noticed a man standing to the side, weeping openly.

"Who is that?" she asked.

"That is Prophet Lut," Grandfather said. "Prophet Ibrahim's nephew."

"Can two prophets live at the same time?" Yasser asked, sniffling.

"Yes," Grandfather said, nodding his head. "Prophet Yahya lived at the same time as Prophet Isa and Prophet Zakariyya; Prophet Shuayb lived at the same time as Prophet Musa and Prophet Harun...."

Zahra felt a bit of peace enter her heart at the thought of there still being a prophet amongst the people who could continue to speak of the message of Allah. She was still hurting from what had happened to Prophet Ibrahim though and was a little surprised at how calm Grandfather was after such a brutal experience.

Yasser was paying attention to Prophet Lut who had now wiped his tears. He sat down on a nearby stone and busied himself with dhikr, waiting for the fire to die down. The crowd also noticed something strange, and a few soldiers went closer to investigate.

Yasser squinted. Could it be? he thought, shaking his head. Or was the smoky air deceiving him? But how? He tugged on Zahra's sleeve and pointed to the figure standing in the fire.

More people were starting to notice. They pointed towards the fire and whispered to each other. The disruption in the crowd caught the King's attention. He raised a hand to order for silence and walked towards the fire. All that could be heard as he moved closer to the dying flames was the clunk of his wooden soles and the chink of his jewellery. He narrowed his eyes in disbelief as a shadowy, smoking figure emerged slowly out of the fire.

The King's eyes widened in shock. **"IMPOSSIBLE!"** he cried out. There, sitting on the edge of the fire, the flames still licking at his clothes, was Prophet Ibrahim – alive and unharmed. As Prophet Ibrahim and King Namrood stood face to face, Yasser could not help but think that it was a face-off between truth against falsehood.

"I know that Allah can do anything," Yasser said, shaking his head in astonishment. "But I never, ever, ever expected that He would make the fire cool for Prophet Ibrahim!"

"This is the most amazing thing ever!" Zahra was jumping up and down, holding on to Yasser's shoulder. "Prophet Ibrahim didn't expect it either; he was actually willing to die for tawheed and he put all his trust and faith in Allah alone!"

The children hugged Grandfather as their relief washed over them. Their celebration was short lived though, because the crowd was growing restless once again.

"This God must be powerful to perform a miracle like that!" one merchant said out loud. "What if Ibrahim's God is true?"

"Perhaps Ibrahim was right all along," another wondered. People began to voice their doubts, some arguing for and others against. They all forgot the King who was watching and listening to their dissent. King Namrood could not bear the embarrassment. These people were supposed to be scared of him and now they barely remembered his presence.

"What sorcery is this?" he shouted, pointing an accusing finger at Prophet Ibrahim.

Prophet Ibrahim stepped forward and calmly replied, "My Lord is the One who gives life and causes death."

King Namrood's jaw clenched and through gritted teeth, he said "I give life and cause death!"

He called for a prisoner to be brought forward. A soldier rushed to the dungeons and returned with a convicted prisoner. He turned to the crowd and proudly announced, "I grant you life, you are free!" Then King Namrood called the soldier forward, as he got closer, King Namrood pulled a diamond encrusted dagger from his belt and stabbed the soldier in his heart. The soldier fell to the ground with a thud. The crowd gasped, and King Namrood announced again, "**I GIVE LIFE AND I CAUSE DEATH !**"

Prophet Ibrahim was not impressed. He looked sadly at the man the King had killed. Life was sacred and not to be played with. However, he had a mission to fulfil and so he posed a second challenge to Namrood: "Indeed, Allah brings up the sun from the east, so bring it up from the west if you can!"

The King was dumbstruck. There was no way he could do what he had been asked to and everyone watching their conversation knew that. Prophet Ibrahim had exposed him in front of all the people. Namrood turned his back and rushed back to his carriage, leaving behind Prophet Ibrahim and the people who were finally beginning to see the truth he had been telling them about for so long.

Grandfather held the children tightly and said in final tone. "Allah does not guide the wrongdoers."

Chapter 12

Yasser and Zahra were buzzing with excitement. They still could not fully believe what they had just witnessed. It had been amazing to see how Allah's Help was always near, even in the most difficult of situations.

Zahra had a niggling doubt at the back of her mind though. "Grandfather," she said, "I thought Prophet Ibrahim was going to die in that fire. Why did Allah not save him until the very end? Why not just save him before instead of allowing him to be treated like that?"

"Many times, Allah will let us go through some hardship so that He can both test us and strengthen us," Grandfather explained. "We need to realise how sincere our trust really is so that we can better understand ourselves. Prophet Ibrahim had faith that Allah's Plan was perfect, even if that meant being burnt in the fire and because of that, he passed his test with flying colours."

Zahra felt a conviction strengthen deep inside her that Allah would always help her, although, perhaps not always in the way she expected. She would work hard to be like Prophet Ibrahim and put her trust in Allah.

"Well Namrood failed his test terribly," Yasser said, with a laugh. "I can't believe he actually thought he was a god!"

Grandfather nodded slowly, but he didn't smile. "When people become more powerful, they start to think that they are responsible for their own success, instead of realising that it all comes from God. That's called **ARROGANCE**. The more they rely on themselves, the more they forget about God. This can become very dangerous if they begin to think they have the power to rule over others and bully them. That's how we get tyrants who try to control their fellow human beings and even kill them."

"I would never be a leader like that," declared Yasser.

"We have to always be careful," Grandfather said. "Arrogance isn't something that only affects leaders; it's a disease any one of us can have even in our ordinary lives." As humans using technology, we have a lot of power, we must be careful to always remember that Allah is the cause of everything;

that is a big part of tawheed.

Yasser and Zahra took a moment to reflect on what Grandfather had said. Did they always remember that Allah was the only One with power?

Yasser broke the silence. "Grandfather?" he asked. "What has all of this got to do with Hajj though?"

Zahra suddenly remembered Mum and her trip. She had been so busy thinking about Prophet Ibrahim that she hadn't thought about Mum for hours!

"Ahhh," said Grandfather. "It has everything to do with Hajj. Come on, let me show you." They climbed back onto the rug together. "To Makkah!" Grandfather instructed.

The rug floated up into the air and Yasser and Zahra could see the whole city spread out below them. Far below, they saw Prophet Lut bidding farewell to Prophet Ibrahim as he left the city with a small group of followers. Zahra wondered where he was going and hoped it would not be the last time they saw him.

Chapter 13

As they zoomed down over the city of Makkah, Yasser, Zahra and Grandfather got a good aerial view of the whole of Masjid al Haraam, the Sacred Mosque of Makkah that housed the Kaaba.

"Look at that giant clock!" Yasser exclaimed, pointing to the towering structure on one side of the mosque. "Have we travelled to the future?"

"No!" retorted Zahra, giggling. "Look at the date on it, we're in the present day!"

The rug paused in its descent, bobbing gently above the Masjid. The pilgrims they had seen leaving the miqaat had now arrived at the central point of Hajj. The Kaaba was the heart and soul of the pilgrimage and an ocean of white flowed around it in tawaf. Although there were people from different countries and different races, they moved as one harmonious body, circling with love and complete devotion. The ambient sound was a melodic symphony of the recitation of Qur'an, whispered prayers and the praise of One God.

Zahra found the tawaf mesmerising. She couldn't stop staring, hypnotised by the white-clad figures moving as if in orbit around the source of energy for their faith – the holy Kaaba. It was a sea of humanity, diverse in culture and background, yet united in purpose.

It was the Kaaba that Yasser focused on - the House of God, draped in black and gold – it was like a magnet that every pilgrim's heart was drawn towards. Yasser felt as if he had arrived somewhere where he was completely safe, as if he had arrived home. His fingers itched to reach out and touch it and noticed that many of the pilgrims seemed to feel the same way. They kept stretching out their hands to stroke the smooth walls of the Kaaba, unable to hold back their love and affection.

Grandfather watched Yasser and Zahra absorb the scene. "As long as a person is looking at the Kaaba, good deeds will be written in their record, and evil deeds will be erased until they turn away their glance from the Kaaba," he said encouragingly. "That is what Imam Baqir (as) told us."

"Just looking at the Kaaba is good for us?" Yasser asked, thinking this sounded too easy.

Grandfather nodded. "Why do you think there is such a great reward just for looking at the Kaaba?"

"Well," Yasser said, turning a pensive gaze back to the holy house, "when I look at the Kaaba, I remember that there is only one God."

"And I love how it is at the centre and everyone moves around it," Zahra added.

"Exactly!" Grandfather said with a smile. "Allah (swt) should be at the centre of our lives; He should be the foundation of every decision we make and every relationship we have. Looking at the Kaaba is supposed to remind us of this." Grandfather waved his hand over the scene below them, "You see children, **TAWHEED IS NOT JUST AN IDEA IN OUR MINDS THAT WE BELIEVE IN. IT IS SOMETHING REAL**. The unity of God is the natural state of the world. Everything is arranged in a way that is directed to God and moving to Him; moving away from God is like swimming against the current. It is only when we are pulled in the direction of God that we find peace through His remembrance."

Yasser and Zahra took a moment to think about what Grandfather had said. What they had seen so far about the way Prophet Ibrahim lived his life began to make more and more sense. They realised that tawheed had been at the core of all his choices and that was why everything about what had happened to him made so much sense.

Yasser wondered whether God was at the centre of his life. He thought about the choices he had made in the past: the times he had care more about his friends than Allah's Pleasure or the times he hadn't considered what Allah wanted and gone ahead to do whatever he felt like. He focused on the Kaaba and whispered a silent prayer: *O Allah, please help me keep You at the centre of my life always.*

Zahra was thinking about how Mum had worked so hard to be able to go for Hajj. She started to see why it was wajib for every person to make the trip if they could afford it. Hajj was a chance for a person to reflect on their life and priorities. It was a physical reminder of the most important thing in the entire universe – tawheed.

Chapter 14

As they continued to watch the pilgrims from their vantage point, Zahra spotted a group who had completed their tawaf. They stopped in front of the Kaaba and offered two rakaats of prayer. As they stood and bowed, a sudden realisation washed over Zahra. The Kaaba is my qibla. She repeated the words in her head, but this time with a new understanding. *Every time I stand for prayer at home or at the mosque or anywhere, I am facing this exact Kaaba that millions of Muslims around the world are also praying towards!* She felt a connection with all her Muslim brothers and sisters everywhere - all facing one direction – worshipping one God. It was impossible to feel alone after realising that; She would only have to stand on a prayer mat and be immediately linked to all the other faithful who were praying at that moment.

She smiled to herself and turned back to look at the small group just in time to see them start to walk to another part of Masjid al Haraam. "Where are they going?" she asked Grandfather, pointing out the small cluster.

Grandfather squinted to spot the people Zahra was pointing to amongst the millions of moving bodies. "Ahh," he exhaled, finally seeing them. "They are headed to perform saee."

"Suh-ee? What's that?" Yasser asked.

"It'll be better if I show you!" Grandfather said, swerving the rug higher into the sky. "Hold on!"

As they flew through the crisp air to the tunnel of light, Zahra secretly hoped that they would see Prophet Ibrahim again. She knew that leaving the King Namrood and the idols worshippers in Babylonia could not have been the end of his story. "Grandfather, where are we going?" she asked.

"Perfect timing!" Grandfather replied, as the rug threw them out at the other end. "You can see for yourself!"

The rug had landed outside a small house in a bustling village. Children laughed and played in the street ahead as their mothers washed their laundry, talking loudly to each other and occasionally calling out to their children to be careful. Yasser was tempted to join the children in their carefree play. However, he noticed that there was a lady sitting outside the home they stopped in front of. She didn't join in the chatter and was silently watching the activity around her. Tears shone in her eyes and Yasser wondered why she was so sad.

A few moments after they arrived, she stood up and walked into the house.

"Let's follow her," Grandfather suggested.

They walked from the bright sunlight into the cool shadows of the house, and the children and Grandfather blinked to clear their vision. Before they could see anything, they heard a sound that pierced their hearts – it was a wail that carried the greatest pain.

"Oh, she's crying!" Zahra said, her own eyes beginning to water. "Why is she crying? Who is she?"

They could now see the figure of the woman. She was holding a corner of her shawl to her mouth and weeping into it. The tears flowed down her cheeks, and she looked like she would never stop.

Suddenly a man walked out from an inner room. Both children felt a thrill as they recognized him. It was Prophet Ibrahim! He looked older and had a thicker beard, but he still had the same calm, peaceful look on his face.

"My dear wife." He hugged the woman and rubbed her back as she sobbed into his shoulder. "We must be patient and trust in Allah."

"Prophet Ibrahim is married!" Zahra exclaimed. "Who is she?"

"That is Lady Sarah," Grandfather answered. "She is a pious woman with great character. They have been happily married for many years now."

"But why is she crying if they are happy?" Yasser asked.

"Well, it has been a long time, and they do not have any children," Grandfather said, gesturing at the empty house.

The fact that not having children would cause Lady Sarah so much pain surprised Yasser. He had never thought what it would be like not to have a sister, or what it might be like for Mum not to have them. It was impossible to imagine. Perhaps he had taken having a family for granted.

Lady Sarah wiped away her tears and looked up at Prophet Ibrahim. Yasser and Zahra could see that they loved each other very much. Prophet Ibrahim kept consoling his wife and encouraging her to be patient. Sarah was still hiccupping with sobs, but her face slowly took on a determined look, as if she had come to a decision.

"I want you to marry Hajar," she said. "Perhaps she will give you a son."

Lady Sarah insisted and continued to repeat her request until she convinced him. Yasser and Zahra looked on, impressed with how she wanted Prophet Ibrahim to have children, even if she was not the mother.

Grandfather put his arm around the children, remembering the day each of them was born. He knew they could not understand how precious children were to their parents or how much love Allah put in the hearts of parents, but he prayed that some day they would revisit this story and realise the strength of both Prophet Ibrahim and Lady Sarah in the choices they were making.

"Prophet Ibrahim did marry Lady Hajar," Grandfather told them. "She was a pious woman as well and Allah (swt) blessed them with a beautiful baby boy."

Grandfather put a hand each on Yasser and Zahra's shoulders and turned them gently. A gentle swish of a breeze and a blink of bright light told the children they were moving through time again. When they completed their turn, they were in the same house, but the scene was completely different.

A young woman sat in the room playing with a baby. *That must be Lady Hajar,* Zahra thought to herself. The woman was kissing the baby's face and hands and he gurgled in response. Zahra smiled as she watched them play, a warm feeling spreading through her heart. She thought of how her own mother loved her fiercely. She looked to the other side of the room where Lady Sarah sat, busy sewing baby clothes. She smiled as she watched Lady Hajar and the baby, but it was a sad smile. Zahra made a du'a from deep within her heart that Allah would bless Lady Sarah with a child too.

Just then, Prophet Ibrahim came into the room. He was holding a small satchel of clothes and provisions. Both women in the room looked at him as he walked to where Lady Hajar was. "It's time to leave," he said to her.

Lady Hajar nodded and stood up. She wrapped her baby in a swaddle and followed Prophet Ibrahim outside to where he was loading the satchel onto a camel.

"What's happening?" Zahra asked. "Where are they going?"

"Let's follow them and find out!" Yasser begged.

Grandfather and the children quickly climbed onto the rug, which rose up and floated gently next to the camel. They watched as Prophet Ibrahim helped Lady Hajar mount the camel and handed her the baby. As soon as mother and child were secure, Prophet Ibrahim pulled on the reins of the camel to make it stand and they started their journey. He walked ahead slowly, holding the reins of the animal and they moved through the town, out the city gates and into the desert.

The hours blended into each other, and the children watched time pass as if on fast forward. Day turned into night and then day again, the sun and moon taking turns to cycle through the sky. They passed towns, villages and open-air markets in a blur. Zahra wondered how far they were travelling and where they were headed.

After many sunrises and sunsets, Prophet Ibrahim finally stopped in a deserted valley where a lone tree stood. The noon sun shone harshly over the sands and the tree provided little shade from its heat, but it was the only place to rest. He tied the camel to the tree and helped Lady Hajar and the baby dismount.

"Why has Prophet Ibrahim stopped here?" Yasser wondered.

Zahra looked around. "This place is empty. There are no houses or people. There isn't even any water here. It is just an empty valley in the middle of nowhere!"

Yasser looked around, but apart from the far-off dunes, there was nothing of importance in the plains before them. *Surely, there must be a reason for stopping here*, he thought. *We just can't see it.* And then remembering what he had seen in Prophet Ibrahim's life so far, he added one word. *Yet.*

Chapter 15

After having a simple meal with his family and a short rest, Prophet Ibrahim stood up. He hugged his baby to his chest for a long moment and then kissed his forehead and placed him back into his mother's arms.

"Looks like it's time to leave," Yasser said, clambering back on the rug.

"Wait!" Zahra said, not moving. "I think... Prophet Ibrahim is leaving on his own?" She turned to look at Grandfather who had not moved from his spot, but was concentrating on what was happening.

Lady Hajar seemed to have noticed the same thing. She reached out and pulled at Prophet Ibrahim's arm as he was about to mount the camel.

"Tell me one thing..." she asked, looking at him and then at her baby. **"IS THIS TRULY WHAT GOD HAS COMMANDED?"**

Prophet Ibrahim slowly nodded. Lady Hajar knew that Prophet Ibrahim loved her and their baby very much. She could see from his face that it was very difficult for him to abandon them in this deserted valley. However, she also knew how strong his faith was and she had learned to trust Allah's Will. If this was what God wanted, Lady Hajar was willing to stay. She let go of Prophet Ibrahim's arm.

Prophet Ibrahim mounted the camel, called out his good bye and started to leave. After a few steps, he looked back and said, "I have submitted to the Lord of the Worlds." Then he raised his hands in prayer, "Our Lord! I have settled some of my offspring in a barren valley, near Your Sacred House, our Lord, so that they may establish prayer. So, make the hearts of believing people incline towards them and provide them with fruits, so perhaps they will be thankful."

Yasser gulped. "Did you hear that?" he asked, nudging Zahra.

She nodded, speechless. Why would Allah command a prophet to leave his wife and baby in the desert without water or shelter? It seemed that Allah wanted to emphasize and test Prophet Ibrahim's absolute reliance on Him alone.

"Did you hear how he first mentioned prayer, and then a society and then food to eat last?" Yasser asked. "What a strange way to order things..."

"That is what you were thinking?" Zahra asked, incredulously. "Honestly Yasser, do you always have to think of food first!" And although she couldn't help being amused at Yasser's observation, she had to admit that she was surprised by Prophet Ibrahim's priorities too.

Lady Hajar watched for as long as she could see Prophet Ibrahim and it was only when his camel disappeared over the sand dune in the distance that she sat back down under the lonesome tree. She nursed her baby until he fell asleep and then rested for a while. When the baby woke up again, he was hungry and began to fuss. Lady Hajar tried to nurse him again, but this time she was not able to.

"She must be thirsty herself," Zahra said. "We've been out in the desert heat for hours."

Lady Hajar tried to distract the baby, singing to him, rocking him and playing with him, but his cries grew louder as the hours passed. She stood up, shielding her eyes from the blazing sun, as if trying to search into the distance for a clue about how to get some water.

A nearby hillock caught her attention. "My love," she said to her baby. "I will have to leave you for a while. Perhaps if I climb that hill, I can get a better view of the valley and see if there is any water nearby."

Yasser and Zahra looked on as Lady Hajar carefully placed her baby at the foot of the tree. She took one loving look at him and then ran to the hill and started climbing it. Zahra was amazed at the strength of Lady Hajar in leaving her child behind, but she also loved how Lady Hajar had chosen to do something. She hadn't sat around, feeling sorry for herself and waiting for someone to help her; she had taken matters into her own hands and decided to figure out a solution for herself and her baby.

The time-travelling trio watched as Lady Hajar reached the summit and scanned the desert plains.

"I think she spotted something!" Yasser exclaimed in relief. "Looks like it's over there on the other mountain."

"Yes! I see her running there now!" Zahra said as Lady Hajar ran to the next mountain.

They watched her climb to the top and waited to see what would happen. Lady Hajar paused for bit, a tiny figure in the distance.

"She is running back!" Zahra said.

"Did she get any water?" Yasser asked, narrowing his eyes.

"No....I don't think so," Zahra replied with disappointment as she saw Lady Hajar running empty handed. Instead of coming back to where they were standing with the baby, Lady Hajar paused at the top of the first hill and looked back to where she had just come from.

"What is she doing?" Yasser tried to figure out as she ran again to the second hill. He was afraid she would get exhausted and not make it back to her baby. Grandfather was holding his arms over the baby, trying to provide some extra shade, even though he knew it made no difference. He just wanted to be doing something as well.

"Maybe she keeps spotting something on the other side," Zahra said, feeling desperate. "Like a mirage."

"But how long will she be able to run for?" Yasser asked, counting four times already. "And why does she go back again and again when she's already seen there's nothing there?"

"It's because she's a mother and she can't give up any chance, no matter how small, to get water for her baby," Zahra said with awe. Lady Hajar continued to run back and forth, moving between hope and fear. Even though she was thirsty and tired, she did not give up. She had run back and forth seven times when suddenly, a rumble passed through the ground. They all felt it and Lady Hajar must have as well because she stopped running and looked down to where they were standing near her baby.

"What's going on?" Zahra asked, looking down as the small pebbles near their feet began to jump.

Before anyone could answer, a jet of water shot up from the ground near the baby's feet. Lady Hajar came running down the mountain with a worried look, but when she saw the water, a smile broke across her face. She fell to her knees near her child, her eyes wet with grateful tears, thanking Allah for His kindness and generosity. Then she cupped the cool water in her hands and fed her baby first before taking sips herself.

"Allah never leaves the ones He loves," Grandfather said in a matter-of-fact tone. "This miraculous water is called **ZAMZAM** and it still flows in Makkah to this day."

"Are we in Makkah?" Zahra asked, looking around. This desert looked nothing like the Makkah they had seen with restaurants, hotels and the giant clock.

Grandfather nodded. "Yes, this is the land that

will become Makkah. Pilgrims will come here to quench their thirst with Zamzam water, and benefit from its healing properties. And those mountains over there that Lady Hajar climbed? They are called **SAFA** and **MARWA**. As part of Hajj and Umrah, pilgrims must copy the actions of Lady Hajar and walk between these two mountains seven times. That is where that group was going after the tawaf."

"Allah must really love what Lady Hajar did to make every Muslim do what she did!" Yasser said.

"Indeed, He did! Allah loves those who are patient and who do their best and then trust Him to do the rest," Grandfather agreed. "Surely the Safa and the Marwa are among the signs appointed by Allah…" he recited from the Qur'an. "The act of walking between them is called **SAEE**."

"Saee?" Yasser repeated. "That's the word you said before."

"Yes, it means 'search', or to move with an aim," Grandfather said.

Grandfather poured Zamzam water into Yasser and Zahra's outstretched palms and they quenched their thirst with the miraculous water. As the crimson sun set, they watched Lady Hajar look after her baby with a peaceful contentment, whispering prayers of love and thankfulness to Allah all the while

"Grandfather, what is Prophet Ibrahim's son called?" Zahra asked.

"Aha!" Grandfather winked. "I have been waiting for you to ask me. That baby is Prophet Ismael!"

"Prophet Ismael?!" Yasser exclaimed making the connection in his mind.

Yasser, Zahra and Grandfather sat on the rug and talked about all they had seen and the lessons they had learned from Prophet Ibrahim and Lady Hajar. Their hearts were bursting with love for this family. They drifted into the most peaceful sleep they had ever experienced.

In the morning, they were woken by the sound of birds flapping and squawking above them. Grandfather looked up and smiled. "These birds are usually found near water in the desert." He said pointing above them.

Grandfather was not the only one to notice these birds. Travellers passing by saw the birds from afar and came closer looking for water. When they found

Lady Hajar and her baby near the water, they asked her if they could drink her water and she agreed.

Grandfather explained how this small stream became the centre of a new town called Makkah. "As generations passed, the small spring grew into a vital oasis, transforming the very landscape around it. Caravans laden with spices, silks, and precious gems made pilgrimages to Zamzam, their weary travellers finding solace in its life-giving waters."

Yasser was amazed to see how the story of Zamzam became a symbol of hope, resilience, and the boundless mercy of the Divine.

Zahra's heart swelled thinking of how Prophet Ibrahim's prayers had been answered.

Chapter 16

"How about we return to present day Makkah?" Grandfather asked the children. "There's something there I want to show you..."

Yasser and Zahra nodded in agreement, wondering what Grandfather had planned for them next. They stood on the emerald green rug and Grandfather helped them wash their faces with Zamzam water. By the time the water on their faces dried, the scene before them had changed, and they were back in present day Makkah! They were in the same spot, but instead of being outside under the open sky, they were indoors under a huge structure. They could see men, women and children walking back and forth in two wide columns.

"Are all these people doing Saee?" Yasser asked, a little confused.

"Yes, that's exactly what they are doing," replied Grandfather. "Copying Lady Hajar to this day."

"But where are the mountains?"

"There are only remnants of the mountains visible now," Grandfather pointed at each end of the long corridors. "A lot of Makkah no longer looks as it did during the time of our prophets, but we are grateful that we are still blessed to know the locations of all our holy sites."

As they explored the area and watched the pilgrims, Zahra could not hold back her surprise at that fact that Zamzam continued to flow, connecting the present to the past. She watched as people from all corners of the globe gathered around the sacred pool, collecting water from the miraculous spring that had transformed a barren desert into a sanctuary of life.

When they went back to the Kaaba, Grandfather had another interesting bit of information to share. "Do you see that semi-circle next to the Holy House?" he asked.

Yasser and Zahra looked at where he was pointing and realised that the tawaf was not a perfect circle as they had assumed. The pilgrims needed to walk around the wall that Grandfather had pointed out, changing the shape of the tawaf into a wonky circle when they did so.

"What's that?" asked Yasser.

"Lady Hajar is buried right next to the Kaaba, and that semi-circle is called Hijr Ismael," Grandfather said.

"Mashallah!" Zahra exclaimed. Her love for Lady Hajar was growing with every new thing she learnt about her. "She must have been an amazing role model for the people to bury her in such an honoured space."

"Let's take a look from the air again," Grandfather said; the rug was still beneath their feet whirling them up and around the Kaaba. Looking down from above, he showed the children how all four corners of the Kaaba pointed to different sides of the world. "This is the Iraqi corner," he said pointing to the corner next to **HIJR ISMAEL**. Then he pointed to a beautiful golden pipe that hung above Hijr Ismael. "Whoever prays under that pipe is guaranteed to have their supplications granted…"

he said wistfully. He showed them the Shami corner and then he stopped above the Yemeni corner next.

"Why is there a crack in the wall there?" Zahra asked. "Did something damage it?"

"Wait!" Yasser gasped as the cogs in his mind turned in double time. "That's where the wall of the Kaaba cracked open for Imam Ali's mother to go in when he was born, right?"

"Yes!" Grandfather replied, enthusiastically.

"Wow!" Yasser exclaimed. He thought about all the prophets and Imams who had lived on the land spread out in front of them. When people walked on the land of Makkah, they could be literally following the footsteps of a Messenger of Allah! How super amazing was that!

Grandfather was slowly bringing the rug around to the fourth and the busiest corner of the Kaaba. Hundreds of pilgrims had stopped there; Yasser and Zahra could not see through the throng at what was causing the pause in tawaf.

What could it be? Zahra thought. *And why is everyone reaching out their hand? What do they want to touch?*

As if reading her mind, Grandfather spoke. "This is where the **BLACK STONE** from heaven is kept. It is the starting point of tawaf."

Zahra held her breath in awe. *A piece of heaven on earth...*

"The Holy Prophet described the black stone as Allah's shrine for all prophets and Imams throughout history."

"No wonder everyone wants to touch it!" Yasser said.

"Imam al-Sadiq said that to caress the black stone is like shaking hands with Allah!" Grandfather said.

"But Allah doesn't have hands!" Yasser protested.

"It's a metaphor, Yasser," Zahra said slowly, rolling her eyes. "It just means that it's like you've pledged loyalty to Him. In the same way Muslims used to pledge loyalty to the Prophet and the Imams."

"Zahra's right," Grandfather said, smiling and ruffling Yasser's hair. "Allah uses many metaphors and examples to make things easy for us to understand."

"Can we go closer to it?" Zahra asked, hoping to be able to get some of the reward that the Prophet and Imam al-Sadiq had mentioned.

Grandfather tried to steer the rug closer, but there were too many people jostling each other for them to reach the black stone. The rug got caught between the arms of a couple of pilgrims and tilted, almost throwing Yasser overboard! Zahra quickly reached out and caught his elbow, heaving him back to the center. Grandfather quickly pulled the rug away from the rush and said, "Imam al-Ridha told us that when it is this busy, waving a hand to it will be the same as touching it."

They all held up their right hands towards the Black Stone and in their hearts each of them made a promise to Allah to worship Him alone.

Yasser remembered that he had some paper and one of his new gel pens with him. He asked Grandfather if they could remain where they were for a while so he could draw the scene below. After he sketched a diagram of the Kaaba, Zahra and Grandfather helped him label it.

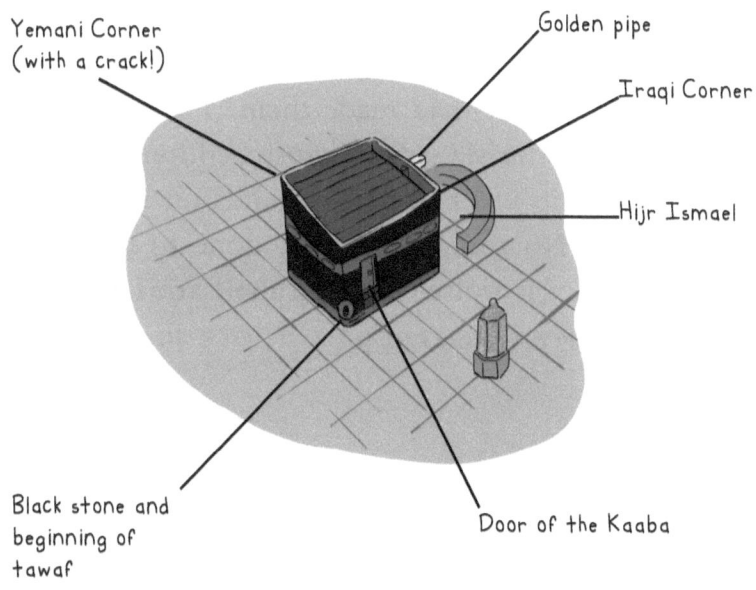

As they were working, Zahra noticed a golden enclosure she had not seen before just a few feet away from the Black Stone. "What's that?" she asked, tugging at Grandfather's sleeve and pointing.

"That is **MAQAM IBRAHIM**. It is said to house the footsteps of Prophet Ibrahim."

"Can we go closer to that?" the children asked in unison.

When they came down to hover over Maqam Ibrahim, Zahra saw the golden footsteps that had been preserved over the centuries. She smiled at the thought that she had been able to actually see the prophet who had made them. There were less people near the Maqam and both children were able to reach out and place their hands on the golden structure. No sooner had they done so than they felt an electric pulse tingle up their arms and with a **ZAP!** they were transported back in time once again.

Chapter 17

It took a few seconds for Yasser and Zahra to recognise that they were in the same valley again. It looked so different to when Prophet Ibrahim had left Lady Hajar and Prophet Ismael there. The water from Zamzam had turned the barren area into a bustling little town. They could still see Mount Safa and Mount Marwa standing tall and in the area in between, there was a small group of houses.

Zahra spotted Lady Hajar outside one of the homes. She was hanging clothes out to dry in the desert sun. Lady Hajar suddenly paused her work and looked directly at her. Zahra gasped. *Can she see me?* she wondered. *Is that even possible?* Lady Hajar narrowed her eyes and then smiled broadly. Zahra realised that she was looking beyond her and into the distance. She turned to look behind her and spotted a figure in the distance coming over the sand dunes and slowly approaching them.

Lady Hajar beckoned to someone inside the house and a young man emerged. Yasser and Zahra looked at each other. Was this...?

"Look at who is coming!" Lady Hajar said, pointing in the distance.

The young man matched her smile when he spotted the figure that was growing larger by the minute. "Go and greet your father!"

"Prophet Ismael has grown into a noble young man!" Grandfather said, as they watched the youth run out eagerly to meet his father. The two hugged tightly and then Prophet Ismael took his father's luggage from him and they began to walk back together. "Prophet Ibrahim loves him very much."

After they had rested and had something to eat, Prophet Ibrahim broke some news to his family. Allah had commanded him to build a house, with his son, on the land. It was to be a holy house where everyone could come and worship Allah and perform pilgrimage. Lady Hajar and Prophet Ismael were delighted to hear the news and they began to prepare for the project immediately.

Yasser looked around. It made perfect sense that Prophet Ibrahim, the Father of Monotheism, should be the one to build the Kaaba. The pieces were fitting together perfectly like a jigsaw puzzle. They all watched as Prophet Ibrahim begin to mark out the area for the Kaaba in the middle of the valley and then clear the space.

"Look how careful Prophet Ibrahim is being about where he is going to build the Kaaba. It's as if he is following very precise instructions!" Yasser was trying to figure out where the plans he was following were drawn.

"The location of the Kaaba is really important!" Grandfather said. "It is directly under **BAYT AL-MA'MOOR**. The angels do tawaf around it in the heavens just as we humans do tawaf around the Kaaba on earth!"

While his father set out the markings for the foundation, Prophet Ismael got to work crafting dark stone bricks and white chalk filling for the fissures. Working together, the father and son team began laying the groundwork, glorifying and praising Allah constantly as they worked.

Yasser was amazed at how simple the Kaaba was. Some handmade bricks laid out in a cuboid and completely empty inside. No gold, silver or marble towers decorated this house, yet it was the most powerful structure in the world.

The children watched again as time passed on a fast reel and after many days, when they laid the last brick, Prophet Ibrahim stood back with his son by his side and sighed with gratitude. They both raised their hands in supplication.

Prophet Ibrahim had tears in his eyes as he raised his face to the skies and called out,

> "OUR LORD! ACCEPT THIS FROM US.
> YOU ARE INDEED THE ALL-HEARING,
> ALL-KNOWING.
> OUR LORD! MAKE US BOTH FULLY
> SUBMIT TO YOU AND FROM OUR
> DESCENDANTS A NATION
> THAT WILL SUBMIT TO YOU.
> SHOW US OUR RITUALS
> AND TURN TO US IN GRACE.
> YOU ARE TRULY THE ACCEPTER OF
> REPENTANCE, MOST MERCIFUL."

Prophet Ibrahim's du'as never ceased to amaze Zahra. It was as if he was seeing something no one else could when asking from Allah. "Did you notice how he did not just pray for himself and his family?" Zahra commented, thinking about her own list of people to pray for. "He's even included the people who would come generations after him. He cares so much about everyone."

"Yeah..." Yasser agreed. "It's as if Prophet Ibrahim is thinking about people in the future and not just those he has been sent to guide in the present! He wants everyone to always be aware of Allah so they can be successful in this world and the hereafter."

"Sshhh..." Grandfather raised a finger to his lips.

"Listen…" he whispered. Prophet Ibrahim had not completed his prayer.

> **"OUR LORD! RAISE FROM AMONG THEM A MESSENGER WHO WILL RECITE TO THEM YOUR REVELATIONS, TEACH THEM THE BOOK AND WISDOM, AND PURIFY THEM. INDEED, YOU ALONE ARE THE ALMIGHTY, ALL-WISE."**

"He is praying for a prophet?" Yasser asked.

"From his descendants?" Zahra finished the question.

As if Prophet Ibrahim's prayer was immediately granted, the rug suddenly jolted, pushing them forward in time. The completed Kaaba stood in the centre of the valley, but they quickly realised that they were not back in the present day. It was still sometime in the past. Idols, much like the ones they had seen in Babylonia, surrounded the Kaaba. Some people were praying to the idols and others walked round the Kaaba without respectful clothing. Yasser and Zahra looked away in shock. The image of idols and the Kaaba together in one place did not make any sense at all! What had happened? Where was Prophet Ibrahim?

Before they had a chance to speak, they heard the sound of large gates being opened and the mingled voices of hundreds of people coming their way. As the sounds got closer, they were able to distinguish the chants of "La illaha illa Allah!" and "Allahu Akbar!" until it seemed that the voices were surrounding them from all directions. Suddenly, the quiet empty space was filled with Muslims and leading them at the forefront, the shining face of Prophet Muhammad dawned on the horizon.

The children cheered with excitement. They finally knew what time they were in!

"Prophet Muhammad was the answer to Prophet Ibrahim's prayer!" Zahra cried excitedly. "He is the messenger that was prayed for!"

Thousands of Muslims peacefully poured into the streets of Makkah and surrounded the Kaaba. The Holy Prophet dismounted his camel and climbed up the steps of the House of God. He announced that all people were safe in the city and then he turned and opened the doors of the Kaaba.

Yasser and Zahra leaned forward as Grandfather took the rug closer to the open doors. They peered inside wondering what could be there since it was supposed to be empty. To their shock and horror, the Kaaba housed hundreds of idols, arranged as if the sacred space was a temple.

Grandfather saw their expressions and quickly explained, "At the time Prophet Muhammad announced that he was the messenger of God and brought the Qur'an, the people in Makkah had gone back to worshipping idols."

Just then they heard a smash and the sound of something shattering. They looked back to see that

Prophet Muhammad was determinedly removing the idols from the Kaaba one by one and dashing them to the floor. Soon the ground was littered with broken pieces of wood and clay.

"This looks so much like the temple we saw in Babylonia!" Yasser exclaimed. "There are so many similarities between Prophet Muhammad and Prophet Ibrahim. They had both been sent to guide people..."

"They both had to deal with idol worshippers and convince them to believe in One God..." Zahra continued.

"They both broke idols and showed the people why they were false..."

"They were both in Makkah…"

"And they both trusted Allah completely in every single thing they did!"

"Amazing!" Grandfather clapped his hands. "That's a lot of good points you have made. In reality, all the prophets, from the time of Adam, came with the same message, to worship the One True God and submit to Him. But Prophet Ibrahim and our beloved Prophet had a special mission to fulfil in their lifetimes."

The three travellers watched as the sun shone brightly down on one of the happiest days for Muslims in their history. The breeze blew with a gentle coolness, birds were chirping and it seemed that the whole world was celebrating the day when the Kaaba was purified and Prophet Muhammad returned to his birthplace as the victor. Not a single drop of blood was shed that day, and the Conquest of Makkah became known as the world's most peaceful takeover of a city.

Chapter 18

"After completing tawaf and saee, the pilgrims cut a small part of their hair or nails and that signifies that they are no longer in the state of ihram." Grandfather explained as they returned to present-day Makkah.

"Is that it? They're done?" Yasser asked, eager to explore the next part of their adventure. "I thought Hajj was longer..."

"Oh, no, that was just the start!" Grandfather laughed. "There is still a lot more they will do in their journey towards Allah (swt). They have now spent a few days in Makkah, praying and preparing for the next stage. Today is the ninth day of Dhul-Hijjah and they now begin the greater pilgrimage!" Yasser and Zahra were intrigued.

"The pilgrims will now enter the state of ihram once again..."

"And the twenty-five things become haram again?" Yasser checked.

"Yes, precisely. They will then leave Makkah in their ihram and travel east to the land of **ARAFAH**."

"Can we go there?" Zahra asked, bursting with excitement.

They held on tight to the rug as it followed the pilgrims draped in white as they poured out of Masjid al Haram. The streets were full of people milling around buses, cars. Everyone seemed stuck in a massive traffic jam and even pedestrians were stuck behind each other, moving slowly in one direction.

"It's going to take aaages for everyone to get to Arafah!" Yasser moaned.

"Hajj is a journey of challenges," Grandfather replied. "Pilgrims have to be very patient and wait in long queues. They have to be kind to their fellow travellers, all while constantly remembering Allah and not getting angry or frustrated."

"Oh wow!" Yasser said, thinking about how hard it was to be always aware of your thoughts and remain patient. If you added waiting for hours under a hot, burning sun, that made it even more difficult!

"Wait a moment," Yasser exclaimed as he realised something. "We have the rug! We don't need to wait in this queue, c'mon Grandfather, let's zoom ahead!"

"That feels like....cheating," Zahra said, worried about being unfair to all the pilgrims who would still have to make the walk.

Grandfather smiled and stroked her head. "It's good of you to think of others, my dear, but we're here for a different purpose than the pilgrims are. I think it'll be okay to go ahead like Yasser suggests."

"Maybe one day we will be the ones walking," Yasser said, nudging Zahra with his elbow to show that he meant well.

She smiled back and said, "InshaAllah!"

Grandfather raced the magical rug over the millions of people flowing in a stream of white, following in the direction they were headed.

"The day of Arafah is considered to be the best and most blessed day in the whole year," Grandfather said, looking down at the pilgrims wistfully.

"Like Laylatul Qadr is the best night?" Zahra asked.

"Exactly! Today is a day when everyone is forgiven and given a chance to start afresh. In fact, it is considered a sin to think that Allah will not have mercy on you if you are in Arafah today!" Grandfather said.

"Are they going to visit a big mosque in Arafah like people do in Najaf and Karbala?" Yasser asked.

"No," Grandfather replied.

"Are they going to walk in a special way like they do in tawaf and saee in Makkah?"

"No."

"Are they going to recite something or pray any special prayers?"

"Nope."

"So...what exactly do people have to *do* in Arafah then?" Zahra wondered.

"The only thing the pilgrims have to do is *be* in Arafah from noon until sunset," Grandfather said.

"JUST BE THERE?" Yasser and Zahra looked at each other with questioning expressions.

"Don't forget, Hajj is not just a physical journey," Grandfather told them. "It is a journey of the heart. When the pilgrims go to Arafah, it is not the land that is their destination, their destination is Allah.

On this day, Allah invites His creation to pause and reflect on their lives and the state of their souls. They can ask for forgiveness; they can think about why they are here on earth and what Allah wants them to achieve in this life. Arafah means to come to know something or recognise something after a process of reflection."

Zahra thought carefully about Grandfather's explanation. So, if a person wanted to come back from Hajj renewed and changed for the better, they needed to spend a good amount of time thinking and reflecting on their lives. She thought about the checklist of prayers and amaals she ploughed through on special nights like Laylatul Qadr. She always tried to fit in as much as she could. *Maybe I need to set aside some time to not just perform acts, but to think about my self and how I can improve on a daily basis.*

Yasser used the afternoon in Arafah to think about who Allah really was to him. He loved how Prophet Ibrahim had questioned things that he saw, that he had reflected and encouraged others to do so. He had really understood and loved the God that he worshipped. The more Yasser reflected on the times Allah had helped him in difficult situations or how Allah had been there for Him whenever he needed, the more Yasser's love for Allah increased. The thought that Allah invited millions of people to Arafah just to forgive them, bless them and grant them mercy made Yasser realise that Allah wanted each and every person to succeed. Yasser smiled broadly. *What a privilege to worship the God of Ibrahim*! he thought to himself.

As the sun began to set, Yasser and Zahra scanned the open plain of Arafah. Each pilgrim had prayed intensely for their needs and fervently asked for forgiveness. Their faces were wet with tears and their expressions softened by humility and contentment. Each pilgrim carried a unique story away from that afternoon. The effect of having dedicated themselves to talking to their Lord was reflected in the deep serenity on many of the faces they saw, as if these people had, for just a moment, been touched by a Divine Presence.

Chapter 19

"Our next stop is…………**MUZDALIFAH**!" Grandfather said, following the current of the sea of pilgrims who had started flowing again in the twilight.

The journey was not too long (especially on the rug!) By the time they landed on the pebbly ground in Muzdalifah, the sky had turned navy blue and black. Yasser, Zahra and Grandfather lay down on their backs on the rug and looked up at the starry sky. The number of stars seemed to mirror the countless tiny stones on the ground.

"Why are so many people collecting pebbles from Muzdalifah?" Yasser asked, turning his head from side to side.

Zahra noticed that the pilgrims were bending down and picking up the small stones. They looked at each one carefully, their lips moving in soft prayers as they gently placed the pebbles into little bags or small packets. "Are these rare stones that people like to take home as souvenirs?" she asked

"They look pretty ordinary to me!" Yasser said,

propping himself up on one elbow and grabbing a handful from the ground.

"Keep those safe, Yasser..." Grandfather said. "You'll find out what's special about them in the next part of our adventure!"

Yasser wasn't quite convinced by this promise, but he poured the stones into his pocket nonetheless. Zahra and Grandfather sat up and picked up stones for themselves as well.

"The people who perform Hajj are Allah's guests." Grandfather said gesturing at the millions on the open plains.

"Just like we were His guests in the month of Ramadhan!" Zahra responded.

"Precisely! If they ask Him for something, He will grant it to them and if they remain quiet, He will speak to them."

"How can you say that?" Zahra asked, thinking that Grandfather must be exaggerating.

Grandfather held up his hands as if he was surrendering. "These are not my words! These are the words of Imam al-Sadiq (as)."

Zahra listened to the soft whispers in the silent night and felt a sense of peace she had not experienced before. Reflection in Arafah had brought a new tranquillity to her heart. She looked at Yasser who was staring up at the sky and could see from his smile that he too was feeling something similar. There was no need to speak. Yasser, Zahra and Grandfather sat in silence enjoying the soothing feeling in their souls, hoping that the Host would speak to them.

After a few minutes, Grandfather reached his hand into his pocket and pulled out the small copy of the Qur'an he always carried with him. He cleared his throat as he opened the page he was looking for. "Surah al Baqarah, verse 198..." he recited. **"WHEN YOU RETURN FROM ARAFAH, THEN REMEMBER ALLAH NEAR THE SACRED**

PLACE AND PRAISE HIM FOR HAVING GUIDED YOU, FOR SURELY BEFORE THIS GUIDANCE YOU WERE ASTRAY."

"Is this the sacred place that the verse is mentioning?" Zahra asked, looking around at all the pilgrims, some praying, some supplicating, and some simply thinking.

"Yes, this is **MASHARIL HARAAM, THE SACRED PLACE,**" Grandfather replied. "Muzdalifah!" he spread out his arms to indicate the land around them.

"I love how Allah guides us so clearly," Yasser said. "He created us with minds to think for ourselves, sent messengers to guide us and gave us the message of the Qur'an!"

"You know, I hadn't realised before," Zahra said, "but you're absolutely right! Prophet Ibrahim showed us that we can know who Allah is by thinking about Him, we followed his example by coming for Hajj and trying to be like him, and all the things we are supposed to do is written down for us in the Qur'an!"

"Everything is connected, and it all leads back to Allah!" Yasser said, delighted at his discovery.

"And that, my dear children, is tawheed," Grandfather said, smiling.

They chatted about all they had seen and the lessons they had learnt so far on their journey. Slowly, the children began to feel drowsy and they cuddled on either side of Grandfather on the soft rug and drifted into a deep sleep under the stars.

Chapter 20

"**PSSST**...Yasser...." Zahra whispered urgently into her brother's ear. "Yasser! Can you hear that?" She shook his arm.

"Mmmm...wha?" Yasser asked, half asleep.

"Yasser, wake up!"

"What is it?" Yasser rubbed his eyes. He was still so sleepy.

"Can you hear that?" Zahra asked. "It sounds like an animal of some sort."

"C'mon Zahra..." Yasser groaned as he sat up. "There's no wild animals in Muzdalifah."

"Well, something is making that sound!" Zahra insisted.

"It's probably Grandfather snoring," Yasser said sleepily. "Let's go back to sleep..."

"I'm not imagining things," Zahra said.

Suddenly a low moaning sound carried through the air, then some bumps and thuds followed by what sounded like a wail.

"That's not an animal," Yasser said, sitting up straight. He was wide awake now. "That sounds like a person."

Yasser and Zahra looked at each other in concern and quickly slipped off the rug to investigate. In the darkness of the night, they almost tripped over the man lying a few feet away before they saw him. He was turned to his side and obviously having a terrible nightmare. Suddenly, he sat up, startling the children who jumped back with collective gasps. As the moon came out from behind some clouds, it shone on his face and Yasser and Zahra recognised him straight away.

"It's Prophet Ibrahim!" Yasser said.

"We've travelled back in time again!" Zahra exclaimed.

Prophet Ibrahim looked around as if he wasn't sure where he was. Then he sighed, recited takbeer and lay back down to sleep. However, it wasn't long before he started tossing and turning again, clearly disturbed by whatever he was seeing in his dreams. Eventually, he woke up again just before dawn, gathered his things and climbed onto his camel, heading out into the desert.

Yasser and Zahra went back running to the rug to wake Grandfather and tell him what had happened.

"We have to catch up with him and see what's going on," Yasser said. "Hurry, Grandfather, we don't have a moment to lose!"

The children scrambled back onto the rug, and they took off to follow the camel and its rider who were already getting smaller and smaller in the distance. Prophet Ibrahim journeyed for many days across the desert. As they saw the Kaaba and the dwellings around it in the distance, Yasser and Zahra realised that he was going to visit Lady Hajar and Prophet Ismael.

Prophet Ismael, though a young man, ran to meet his father in the same way that a child would. They hugged each other tightly and Prophet Ismael kissed his father's forehead in respect. As they sat in the shade of the courtyard of their home, Prophet Ismael brought some fresh milk for his father to enjoy. He knew the journey had been long. His father was getting older and looked tired, as if he had not slept in days.

Prophet Ibrahim's face was weary, and his eyes glazed with unshed tears as he watched the love with which his son served him. After a few moments, Prophet Ibrahim cleared his throat to speak.

"My dear son," he said, considering his words carefully. "I have seen a dream that I must slaughter you. So think about it...what is your opinion?"

Prophet Ismael did not hesitate in replying. **"O MY DEAR FATHER, DO WHAT YOU HAVE BEEN ORDERED TO DO BY ALLAH. YOU WILL FIND ME, INSHALLAH, ONE OF THOSE WHO BEAR PATIENTLY."**

Yasser looked at Zahra in disbelief. "Allah really commanded Prophet Ibrahim to sacrifice his own son?"

"And Prophet Ismael agreed to it?" Zahra was equally shocked. "But it was just a dream! We saw Prophet Ibrahim when he was having it."

"When a prophet has a dream, it is different to when you or I have a dream. Theirs are a form of communication with God," Grandfather explained.

"Prophet Ibrahim would never go against something that Allah has ordered," Zahra realised.

"First he was thrown into the fire, then he was forced out of his town." Yasser was wondering about the tests of Prophet Ibrahim. "Then he couldn't have children and when he finally got a son, Allah asked him to leave his baby in the desert," Yasser's voice became thinner. "And now after his son has survived and grown…now he has to sacrifice him? How much can one person bear?"

"When you say it like that, it sounds awful!" Zahra said. She bit on her lower lip as she worked out something in her mind and when she continued her voice was filled with awe. "But Yasser…think about it. Allah made the fire cool for Prophet Ibrahim, He settled him in a better area so he could preach and gave him a wife that loved him. Then Allah gave him Lady Hajar, who had so much faith and they had a son who is a Prophet. When he left them alone in the desert, Allah took care of them with Zamzam and the place they were in became Makkah! Then He gave them the honour of building the Kaaba," she paused and smiled. "Why are we thinking that Allah would leave them now? He has always been there for them."

Prophet Ibrahim and his family had taught Zahra many lessons, but the one practice she had seen repeated over and over in their lives was the way they submitted to Allah and the way in which He rewarded their obedience with His Love. She was sure this time would be no different.

Chapter 21

Prophet Ibrahim packed a small bag with some dry pieces of bread and a water bag, as well as the things they would need for the sacrifice. Then he set off with Prophet Ismael. Father and son walked in comfortable silence, only pausing to help each other over boulders or down slippery sand dunes. Each of them was having a private conversation with their Lord as they headed towards obedience to His command.

The children and Grandfather eagerly followed on the rug.

"Where are they going?" Zahra wondered.

"To a valley located eight kilometres southeast of the city of Makkah," Grandfather said.

Yasser looked at their shining faces and could not help but remember the time when Imam Husayn had walked his son Ali Akbar into battle. He had dressed Ali Akbar in a suit of armour and wrapped his turban neatly across his head, knowing it would be his final farewell. Prophet Ibrahim had a similar mixture of sorrow and calmness on his face.

"Look!" Zahra cried out, pointing to a figure in a black cloak who had suddenly appeared in front of the two men. "Who could that be?"

"Did you see where he came from?" Yasser asked.

Zahra shook her head. A shiver ran down her spine and the hairs on her arm rose. "I don't like him."

"Oh Ibrahim," the man in black said in a mocking voice. "Where are you going with your son?"

"I am going to sacrifice him," Prophet Ibrahim replied.

The man looked shocked, but there was something about his expression that didn't seem sincere at all. "What crime has he committed?"

"I am doing this on Allah's command."

"But if you kill your own son, you will set a bad example for your followers."

At the mention of his followers, Prophet Ibrahim stopped. A look of worry crossed his face and he looked back towards Makkah and then to the skies, as if thinking about the safety of the connection he had finally made for the people between them and their Lord. He closed his eyes and whispered something under his breath. Then he slowly shook his head, once, twice, and his body relaxed. When he opened his eyes, the worry had been replaced by a confidence. He bent down and picked up some stones from the ground, hurling them at the cloaked man. "Get away from here!" he shouted before taking Prophet Ismael's hand and walking forward with determination.

The cloaked man made an angry sound and backed away, vanishing as suddenly as he had appeared.

"Wait, what..." Yasser looked around. "Where did he go?"

Even as the children were wondering how this strange person was coming and going, they noticed him standing further ahead, waiting for Prophet Ibrahim again.

"How is he doing that!" Yasser exclaimed.

Grandfather simply urged the rug ahead so they could see the second encounter between the man and the two prophets. As they neared, they saw that the man looked different. His face was darker, his expression not so friendly and the folds of his black cloak were swirling madly in the desert wind.

"Oh Ibrahim! What will the people say when they hear what you have done?" he demanded. "How will you explain it to them?"

Prophet Ibrahim drew a deep breath. As he exhaled, he shouted **"BISMILLAH, ALLAHU AKBAR!"** throwing more stones at the man. The man cried out in frustration and wrapped his cloak around himself, vanishing in the cloud of dust and smoke.

They walked for a few more minutes, before the

voice of the man stopped them for a third time. It came from the side and when the children turned with Prophet Ibrahim to look, they saw that the cloaked man was now a towering figure, he was obviously angry and when he spoke, his voice was harsh and boomed across the desert. Zahra shuddered and quickly moved behind Grandfather. She did not like this person at all.

Prophet Ibrahim, however, stood tall and did not even flinch.

"Oh Ibrahim! Look at your son's beautiful innocent face!" He pointed a long bony finger at Prophet Ismael. "How can you put him to death? What kind of father kills his own son? Have you no heart?"

Prophet Ibrahim looked at Prophet Ismael. His face softened with the love he had for him. "I do love you, my son," he said. Then he turned back to the cloaked stranger whose face was breaking into a smile that looked more like a sneer. "But I love Allah more! And I trust Him completely!" This time, Prophet Ibrahim grabbed an even larger handful of stones from the ground and began pelting the man, one stone at a time, until he fled into the winds, shrieking in frustration and anger.

"Who was that?" Zahra asked, still trembling.

"Where did he come from? And how does he know Prophet Ibrahim?" Yasser added. He reached out and took Zahra's hand to comfort her. He knew she didn't like it when people were loud and aggressive.

"Well, that wasn't really a man..." Grandfather

explained. "That was Shaitan himself, trying to tempt Prophet Ibrahim to forget about his love and trust in Allah and to stop him from obeying this command from Him."

"Whaaaaaaat?" Yasser and Zahra looked at Grandfather in disbelief.

"That was Shaitan!" Yasser looked gobsmacked. "He came personally to Prophet Ibrahim!"

"Why now though?" Zahra wondered. "He's never come before at the other times when Prophet Ibrahim was being tested."

"Good question!" Grandfather said, as the rug followed the prophets on their journey. "With every test Prophet Ibrahim passed, his faith grew stronger. Shaitan couldn't bear to see him succeed so well. That's why he was confident he could mislead him when it came to this hardest test of all."

"He didn't count on how strong Prophet Ibrahim's love for Allah was!" Zahra said, smiling.

"Yes, Shaitan is very clever, but he cannot actually make us do anything. He only whispers and suggests things. He knows our soft spots and the things we are attached to, so he tries to use those to persuade and trick us. When we realise that we are in control of our own actions, then we can easily realise what his whispers are and refuse to listen to them."

"That's exactly what Prophet Ibrahim did," Zahra said, thinking back to what they had witnessed. "He took a few moments to think and once he recognised it was Shaitan the first time, he didn't even listen to him the second and third time."

"But why throw stones at him?" Yasser wondered. "It's not like those would hurt him."

"The stones represented the strength of Prophet Ibrahim's faith," Grandfather replied. "They show that Prophet Ibrahim was willing to fight against Shaitan with whatever he had at hand. When Shaitan who is our open enemy attacks us, it is not a time to try and reason with him or discuss the matter. It is a time for struggle. This is the inner battle that our Prophet has taught is the **GREATER STRUGGLE – JIHAD AL AKBAR**."

"Oh, remember the time we decided to give all our Eid money to charity?" Yasser asked Zahra.

"Yeah, but then we decided to only give away a few coins, so we could get something for ourselves too...because we had been so good all Ramadhan."

"Do you think that Shaitan might have convinced us not to give all the money away?" Zahra asked.

"I don't know..." Yasser admitted. "But the next time I decide to do something for the sake of Allah, I am going to rush to do it quickly before anything or anyone tries to change my mind!"

"Shaitan will always try to convince us not to do something that takes us close to Allah," Grandfather said. "Or convince us to do less than we should. Especially when it comes to prayer and our duties towards our Lord."

Zahra thought about all the times she had got distracted on her way to pray and ended up praying late, sometimes just a few minutes before qadha. She made a silent promise to herself to watch out more carefully for the whisperings of Shaitan.

Yasser pulled out the pebbles he had picked in Muzdalifah from his pocket. "Prophet Ibrahim threw stones at him..."

Zahra made the connection too. "Do pilgrims throw the pebbles from Muzdalifah at Shaitan?" she asked.

Grandfather smiled. "Yes, do you remember how the pilgrims were thinking carefully when they chose the pebbles?"

"Hmmm," Zahra said, recalling the scene.

"They were thinking about the sins they had committed and the times that Shaitan had deceived them. In the next stage of Hajj, they will copy the actions of Prophet Ibrahim and throw those stones at the three places that we saw Shaitan appear, declaring him as their enemy and making an intention never to fall into his trap again."

Chapter 22

When the children, Prophet Ibrahim and Prophet Ismael arrived at the valley that Grandfather had mentioned, they stopped.

"Does this place have a name?" Zahra asked, looking around at the empty land.

"Yes, this blessed valley is called Mina," Grandfather replied.

Prophet Ismael turned to his father. He was calm as he spoke. "Please Father, tie my hands and feet so that I do not flinch when you sacrifice me."

Prophet Ibrahim placed a hand on his son's shoulder. He nodded and added, "I will also tie a blindfold over my eyes so that my hand does not falter when I see your beautiful face."

"Look at how eager they both are to please Allah," Zahra said. "They will do anything to make sure they carry out Allah's command properly!"

Prophet Ibrahim opened the bag and took out some rope, a cloth for his blindfold, and a sharp knife. He hugged and kissed his son on both cheeks and then gently bound his hands and feet, preparing himself for the biggest sacrifice anyone could imagine. After he finished, he knelt beside his son, tied the cloth over his own eyes and picked up the knife he had placed nearby. He whispered the name of Allah and placed his other hand on Prophet Ismael's shoulder.

"Oh, I cannot bear to watch!" Zahra cried out, hiding her face in Grandfather's sleeve and praying desperately to Allah to relieve Prophet Ibrahim of this sacrifice.

Yasser wanted to be brave, but he covered his eyes with his hands as well. Even as he prayed for some miracle to help Prophet Ibrahim pass this test, he thought about how he could not sacrifice watching his favourite TV programme when it was time for prayer, or how much he complained when he had to give up food for a few hours in the month of Ramadhan. This was a level of sacrifice that was beyond imagination.

A few moments passed and the silence was unbearable.

"Is it over?" Zahra whispered, her eyes damp.

"It is over," Grandfather said. "Open your eyes."

Zahra looked up at him in surprise. Was he smiling? She whipped around to view the scene and saw that Prophet Ibrahim had lowered his blindfold and was looking equally shocked. In front of him was a ram that he had just sacrificed, and Prophet Ismael stood next to him, safe and sound.

"It was just a test!" Yasser said, jumping up and down with joy. "Allah was just testing Prophet Ibrahim to see whether he would really obey Him!"

Grandfather nodded, beaming . "Allah wanted history to record how much Prophet Ibrahim loved him. He was always going to replace Prophet Ismael with an animal from heaven ."

Yasser and Zahra cheered at the sight of father and son embracing each other and then falling into sajdah to thank Allah for His Love and Mercy. They had passed the test with flying colours!

"Today is the day of Eid!" Grandfather said, pulling Yasser and Zahra to his chest for a tight hug. "Allah even celebrates Prophet Ibrahim's obedience in the Qur'an!" He pulled out the sacred book, kissing its spine before opening it to the verse he wanted. "When Ibrahim's Lord tested him with certain commandments, which he fulfilled; He (Allah) said, 'I will make you a leader of people'."

"Oh maaan," Yasser said in admiration. "Allah (swt) really tested Prophet Ibrahim a lot."

"That's the only way to grow and achieve higher levels in anything," Grandfather replied.

Yasser had always assumed that as he grew older, his faith would naturally grow stronger just like Mum's and Grandfather's. *Have they been tested to reach where they are?* he wondered. *Has Allah ever tested me?* He knew he had never faced anything as challenging as Prophet Ibrahim's tests so he quickly thanked Allah for giving him such a comfortable life, but he was a little worried too.

"Grandfather," he asked. "What if we don't have any tests in our life?"

Zahra nodded. She had been thinking along the same lines it seemed. "Or what if..." she continued. "We can't pass the tests we get?"

Grandfather laughed. "Oh, my dears. Allah (swt) Loves you more than anyone ever can. He never gives anyone a test unless He first gives them the ability and strength to pass it. The only reason someone might fail a test is if they listen to Shaitan who tries to tell them they can't do it – just like he tried to with Prophet Ibrahim. We have to make choices every day, over time we become the result of the choices we make."

"And we have to make sure we make the right choices, and do the things that Allah would be pleased with..." Yasser said, thinking aloud.

"That's absolutely right!" Grandfather said, enthusiastically nodding. "One of the best ways to do that is to take account of our actions and thoughts every night before going to sleep."

"That makes a lot of sense," Zahra agreed. "I think this is something we can work on together, right?" she asked Yasser.

Yasser nodded. Yasser and Zahra often made decisions together – sometimes because they had to agree on something, like which movie to watch, and sometimes because they needed each other's help, like advice about friends or just issues in life! They were thankful to have each other. Now more than ever, they were realising how amazing it is to have someone else look out for you at the times you might get distracted or forget to stop and think about what choice to make. This would definitely require team work just like Prophet Ibrahim and Prophet Ismael had done in building the Kaaba and even in presenting their sacrifice to Allah.

Chapter 23

Yasser, Zahra and Grandfather flew through the tunnel of light and emerged whizzing above crowds of pilgrims. No matter how many times they time travelled, Yasser and Zahra could never get used to the thrilling feeling that rushed through their bodies! They were now back in present day Mina! Rows of tents covered the land as far into the distance as they could see. Grandfather guided the rug towards a huge stone structure where hundreds of thousands had gathered, all throwing their stones and shouting, **"BISMILLAH, ALLAHU AKBAR!" IN THE NAME OF ALLAH! ALLAH IS THE GREATEST!**

Yasser pulled out the pebbles from his pocket and carefully gave some to Zahra and some to Grandfather. Blocking out the noisy crowd below, Zahra silenced her mind and focussed on each pebble, labelling each with a bad habit that she wanted to get rid of. She prayed with all her heart for Allah's help to stay away from all the things He did not like.

Yasser's strategy was more aggressive. He was on attack mode and was flinging each pebble with all the energy he could muster. "Take that, you evil Shaitan!" he yelled, as he threw the stones. "And that! And stay away from me!"

Grandfather was quiet, but he had a look of determination as he threw his stones. This was a personal journey for each of them, just as it was for each of the millions of pilgrims below them.

When they had finished their stones, Grandfather steered the rug to follow those pilgrims who had completed the stoning and headed to sacrifice their animals.

"What do they do with all the meat?" Yasser asked.

"It's shared out amongst the poor and needy," Grandfather replied.

"Where are those people going?" Yasser asked, noticing a queue of male pilgrims that was forming to one side.

"Why is it only the men going there?" Zahra asked, looking in the direction Yasser was.

"They are going for **HALAQ**," Grandfather replied. "They will shave their heads. The ladies will only trim some of their hair or nails."

"Look!" Zahra pointed to the man at the front of the line. "He's just about to have his done!"

They watched as the young man's thick hair fell to the floor revealing the pure smooth skin underneath.

"As the pilgrims get their heads shaved, they make an intention to purify themselves and rid themselves of every bad characteristic. They pray to be as pure and clean as the day they were born," Grandfather explained.

"And now everyone looks even more alike," Yasser observed, as the young man who had just shaved his hair joined the others who had already had their **HALAQ** done and was immediately lost in the crowd.

"Oh my goodness!" Zahra yelped before she burst into a fit of giggles. "I just realised what Mr Rayyan meant when he explained why he was bald!"

"Ohhhh!" Yasser said joining in the giggles.

Meanwhile, Grandfather scanned the crowd keenly, his forehead narrowing in concentration as if he was searching each face for someone in particular.

"Grandfather?" Zahra said, jolting him from his thoughts. "I think that man has gone..."

"Are you looking for Mum?" Yasser asked. It would be like looking for a grain of sand on a beach.

"No." Grandfather smiled, but it was sad smile. "On a day like today, when all the Muslims come together, I miss Imam Mahdi even more. Traditions tell us that the Imam of our Time comes for Hajj every year and he is amongst the crowd. It is comforting to know that he is here with his ummah, but I wish I could see him and perform Hajj with him." Tears welled up in Grandfather's eyes as he spoke.

Zahra thought about how amazing it would be to someday perform Hajj with the Imam who could guide them through every stage. That would be a dream come true. *Please come soon*! She whispered in her heart.

They watched as the pilgrims finished the two rites of Hajj, each of them secretly still looking for one face that might stand out with its light and beauty. As people completed their sacrifices and halaq, they began to leave the area.

"Where is everyone going now?" Yasser asked. "What's the next step of Hajj?"

"Now they will return to Makkah to perform tawaf, saee, and then another tawaf," Grandfather replied.

"All over again?" Yasser asked. This was unexpected.

"Well, yes," Grandfather replied, "but see if you notice anything different this time around..." He grasping the front two corners of the rug like reins on a horse and steered it in the direction of Makkah.

Yasser spotted the tall minarets of Masjid al Haram rising in the distance. Memories of Prophet Ibrahim came flooding back to him. How brave he had been to leave Lady Hajar and baby Prophet

Ismael in this land when it was still barren and deserted. What would he say if he could see, thousands of years later, how his prayers had been answered and how millions of people each year followed in his footsteps submitting to the One true God. How happy he would be!

The pilgrims poured into the Sacred Sanctuary from all sides. Zahra remembered the Conquest of Makkah and how the Muslims returned to the Kaaba victorious.

"Wait, why are they not wearing their ihram anymore?" Yasser asked.

"After they perform the halaq, the pilgrims are no longer in the state of ihram," Grandfather said. "They can now freshen up and change their clothes. But that's only one of the things that's different."

Yasser and Zahra kept their eyes peeled for any other differences they could spot. As the rug flew over the grand entrance, the radiant Kaaba came into view. No matter how many times Zahra saw the Kaaba, it never failed to take her breath away. She drank in its beauty with her eyes and that was when she noticed the second difference.

"Grandfather! The cloth of the Kaaba! It now has a white strip at the bottom!"

"You're right, Zahra!" Grandfather said, smiling. "The cloth of the Kaaba is called the **KISWA** and verses from the Qur'an are woven into it with gold thread. Every year when the pilgrims leave Makkah and head to Arafah, the kiswa is changed!"

The air was thick with the scent of musk and incense, mingled with the subtle aroma of sandalwood rising from the fresh Kiswa. Yasser and Zahra noticed that the pilgrims were different too;

not just their clothes but their behaviour as well. As they circled the Kaaba once again, many of their heads were lowered in reverence to Allah (swt), their faces shining with sincerity and love. The past few days had been an internal journey of purification for most of them; it seemed each of them was now determined to improve and keep the peacefulness they had found through connection to Allah (swt) alive in their hearts.

When they shared their thoughts with Grandfather, he smiled broadly. "And that is the most important difference of all!"

Chapter 24

The crimson sun began to set over the valley of Makkah. Grandfather explained to the children that Makkah was the land of safety and security. All kinds of violence were forbidden in it and even a fly was safe from harm within its boundaries. Yasser and Zahra felt safe in the embrace of the Blessed City.

I could stay here forever, Zahra thought to herself with a satisfied sigh. Which is why she was surprised to notice that people were leaving once again in droves. "Why is everyone leaving Makkah in such a rush again?" she asked.

"They must now spend the eleventh and twelfth days of Dhul Hijjah in Mina," Grandfather answered. "And while they are there, they will stone the three Shaitans again."

Now it was Zahra's turn to be confused. Why were they repeating everything again? This time she decided not to ask Grandfather but to try and observe first and see if she could understand the reason for herself.

Against the backdrop of the arid Arabian desert, the endless rows of stark white tents in Mina looked like pearls strewn across golden sands. The fabric of the tents fluttered gently in the breeze and the atmosphere crackled with the energy of the millions gathered in them.

Yasser, ever curious for details, asked, "Grandfather, can we land and walk around to see inside the tents?"

"Yes, of course!" Grandfather replied, finding a safe place to land. They got off the rug and began walking between the tents recognising the flags from different countries around the world.

"Look, Zahra! That's the flag of Pakistan! I would recognise the green background and white crescent anywhere!"

"And right next to it is the Spanish Flag!" Zahra said, pointing to the vibrant yellow and red fabric.

The following two flags had the broad black stripe of Tanzania and the simple red dot of Japan. "This looks like a United Nations meeting!" Zahra exclaimed.

"Or the World Cup!" Yasser chuckled.

"You're both right!" Grandfather agreed. "Muslims from all over the world gather during the Hajj. They use this time in Mina to get to know each other and discuss important issues facing the Muslim community."

A roar of laugher erupted behind them, its contagious nature made Yasser and Zahra instinctively giggle. "Let's see what's going on!" Yasser said, not wanting to miss out on the fun.

They followed the happy sound to a large tent nearby. Yasser and Zahra quickly realised that the pilgrims in this tent were not all from the same country; the colour of their skin, the clothes they wore and the languages they spoke were all beautifully varied. They were communicating in a mixture of broken English and sign language while attempting to cook a meal together.

"Zis macaroni ghar matbukh!" a bald man with a fury box beard said to the group standing over a large cauldron.

Everyone looked back at him confused, so he picked up a piece of pasta from the pot and pretended to eat it, then he pretended to collapse to the ground, moaning and rubbing his rounded belly as if he had terrible tummy pains.

"I think he is saying that the pasta isn't cooked properly!" Yasser said between giggles.

The other pilgrims laughed heartily when they also finally figured out what he was trying to say. It was as if they were all playing a game of charades! The pot continued to bubble and the group now added more ingredients. A tin of tomatoes from a Brazilian boy, some spices from an Indian lady and cheese from an Iranian pilgrim. Yasser and Zahra thought the meal was going to be as vibrant as the different cultures around them.

"Now I see why the pilgrims stay in Mina again," Zahra said. "It's a chance for people to get to know each other."

"Precisely! The importance of creating bonds of love within the Muslim community is critical," Grandfather said, reaching for his Qur'an. He flipped the pages to Surah Hujarat and recited,

"O HUMANITY! INDEED, WE CREATED YOU FROM A MALE AND A FEMALE, AND MADE YOU INTO PEOPLES AND TRIBES SO THAT YOU MAY GET TO KNOW ONE ANOTHER. SURELY THE MOST NOBLE OF YOU IN THE SIGHT OF ALLAH IS THE ONE WHO HAS THE MOST TAQWA. ALLAH IS TRULY ALL-KNOWING, ALL-AWARE."

"If Allah wanted, He could have made us all the same," Yasser observed. "But it is much more interesting to be different and diverse."

"And the thing that makes us better than others in Allah's eyes is how much faith and sincerity we have, not the colour of our skin! That's the lesson ihram has taught me," Zahra added.

As the children caught up with Grandfather about what they had observed and learnt, the energised group finished their meal. They then began debating the correct way to eat baklava.

Laughter erupted once again as the Indian lady dipped the nutty treat into milky tea and the man with the fury box beard looked as if he was going to faint at the sight! Yasser thought it looked delicious! Between sharing food and laughter, the group also talked about how to keep on holding onto their re-energized faith when they went back home.

"Here good...home hard!" one of the men said with exaggerated gestures. He clenched his fist tight to show how difficult it was. Everyone nodded in agreement.

"This time in Mina is a great opportunity for the pilgrims to reflect on the journey they have made so far. Now that their sins have been forgiven, many of them will make promises to Allah to improve and try to live a life centred around tawheed," Grandfather explained.

"Is this why they stone Shaitan again?" Zahra asked.

"Exactly! Victory should not cause you to relax, because that's when Shaitan attacks again. He never gets tired of trying to mislead us, so we must never get tired of fighting against his whispers," Grandfather said. "And now that they have carried out the pilgrimage of Hajj and walked the footsteps of the chosen servants of Allah (swt), each of these pilgrims has a new responsibility to keep improving themselves every single day."

Chapter 25

After spending a couple of nights in Mina moving around the tents and learning something from the many different individuals there, Yasser and Zahra joined the pilgrims as they returned to Makkah as Hajjis – people who had completed the Hajj. The Hajjis hugged to congratulate each other and prayed to Allah that their pilgrimage had been a successful one and that their efforts had been accepted.

However, even as they celebrated, a silent sadness hung in the air as they prepared to perform their final tawaf. They knew this was goodbye and for some of them it might be their final one. No one knew who would be able to make it back again to be blessed with the sight of the House of Allah.

This time Yasser and Zahra chose to get down from the rug and join the crowd on foot. They let themselves be carried along with the current of bodies moving in harmony round and round the central point of the Kaaba. The marble beneath their feet was cool as they walked the path of generations before them. With a deep sincerity, they circumambulated the Kaaba, promising that they would follow the example of Prophet Ibrahim and keep Allah (swt) at the centre of their lives. Yasser and Zahra had fallen in love with Makkah and the bitter-sweet farewell made them sad too.

After seven rounds of the Kaaba, Grandfather led Yasser and Zahra to Maqam Ibrahim. "Let us recite two rakaahs of prayer here," he said, looking up at the sky that was now painted in rich hues of purple and gold. "It will soon be time for Maghrib."

"Does this mean it is time to go home?" Zahra asked sadly. Her heart felt heavy in her chest.

"Not just yet!" Grandfather said, with a twinkle in his eye. "No Hajj is complete without one more special ingredient!"

Before Yasser and Zahra could ask any more questions, the takbir of adhaan echoed throughout Masjid al Haram.

"ALLAHU AKBAR!" The muadhin's voice sparked an electric energy in their souls. Allah really is the Greatest, Yasser thought, closing his eyes and recalling how Allah had made the fire cool for Prophet Ibrahim.

It was astonishing how the millions standing around the Kaaba had immediately fallen silent, submitting in unity to the command to pray. There was an anticipatory stillness everywhere, as everyone faced the Kaaba waiting for the prayer to start.

"ASH HADU AN LA ILLAHA ILLAH ALLAH!"

Zahra saw the amazing display of monotheism all around her. It didn't matter who you were or where you came from; in front of Allah, you were simply a servant created to worship Him. The Kaaba is a real symbol of the constant eternality of Allah.

There's only one God, she said from the bottom of her heart, closing her eyes and allowing the words to sink in deeply.

"ASH HADU ANNA MUHAMMADAN RASULLULLAH!"

As the muadhin said the statement of witnessing prophethood, Yasser and Zahra felt a tingling breezy whoosh go past their ears. They quickly opened their eyes and found themselves in front of the majestic green dome in Madina!

Grandfather's gleaming face was smiling back at them.

"Imam al-Baqir tells us that people have been commanded to perform tawaf around the Kaaba and after that to visit the Ahlulbayt and declare their allegiance and offer their help to them. So, you see, no Hajj is complete without visiting the Prophet (saw)."

Yasser and Zahra looked around at the stunning masjid, trying to absorb every moment of history that flashed before their eyes. Grandfather took them inside and showed them the Prophet's house, which was right next to the house of Lady Fatima and Imam Ali (as).

"This is the door the Angel Jibrael would enter from to reveal the Qur'an to Prophet Muhammad," Grandfather pointed out. "And here is the **MIMBAR** where the Prophet gave speeches and that is the **MIHRAB** where he led prayers."

Yasser remembered his favourite stories of how Imam Hasan and Imam Hussain would sit on the mimbar on the Prophet's lap and climb on him when he prayed in the mihrab.

"What is that over there?" Zahra asked, pointing to what looked like a raised platform.

"That is where some of the companions of the Prophet used to live."

"But it's so small!"

"Yes, some of the people who joined the Prophet gave up everything including their wealth and homes to be with him. They were willing to make do with only the basics of life in order to be next to the Prophet."

"Perhaps they felt richer than anybody, just being in the company of the Prophet..." Zahra thought she would feel rich, but she wasn't sure she would be able to live in just a small room shared with others.

"Why is the colour of the carpet different here?" Yasser asked, noticing that a section of the scarlet carpet had given way to a mint green one.

"The green carpet marks out the space between the Prophet's house and the mimbar. It is said that in this area lies a piece of heaven," Grandfather replied.

"**A PIECE OF HEAVEN**?" Yasser asked. "For real?" he could not believe what he was hearing.

Grandfather nodded.

"That must be why they call it **THE CITY OF LIGHT**," Zahra said. "It's filled with blessings in all its spaces!"

They recited two rakaats of prayer on the green carpet and prayed for the chance to visit the piece of heaven they were standing on again. They were surrounded by the gentle hum of recitation from the Qur'an. People all around them were paying their respects to the Father of the Ummah. Zahra felt a deep gratitude to be a follower of the Prophet and the Ahlulbayt; she knew that she had to thank Allah for His guidance otherwise she might have been amongst those who didn't know!

Grandfather raised his hands in prayer and said out loud:

"OH ALLAH! SEND YOUR BLESSINGS ON PROPHET MUHAMMAD AND HIS FAMILY IN THE WAY THAT YOU SENT YOUR BLESSINGS ON PROPHET IBRAHIM AND HIS FAMILY. SURELY YOU ALONE ARE THE PRAISEWORTHY AND THE ONE THAT RESPONDS."

When they had completed their prayers and du'as, Yasser and Zahra sat down with Grandfather and worked to draw a map of everything they had seen. They wanted to take advantage of the fact that they were in a blessed land and that they could still feel the energy of the past they had witnessed reverberating in the present. They did not want to forget this moment and tried to capture it on paper as best as they could.

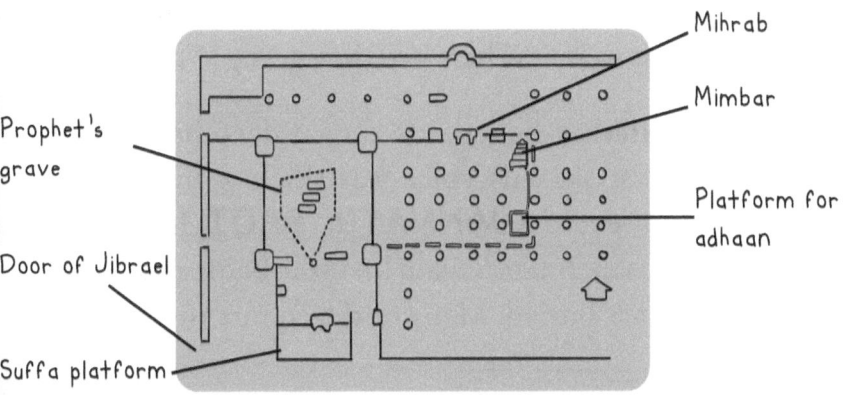

Chapter 26

After spending as much time as they could inside Masjid al Nabawi and soaking in the peaceful atmosphere, they finally emerged and began to stroll through the vast courtyard. People walked around, some were sitting and reciting Qur'an, others were talking and simply enjoying being in the presence of the Prophet.

"It feels so good to be near our Prophet even if we are separated from him by time," Zahra said. "I can't imagine how the companions who got to see him and spend every day with him must have felt."

Yasser was looking around, trying to figure out the layout of the courtyard so he could draw another map and mark any interesting features to remember. He noticed a gated graveyard a few hundred metres away. Small groups of people were heading back and forth to it. "Where are they going?" he asked.

Grandfather sighed. He took a deep breath and when he spoke, his voice was thick with sadness. "That graveyard is **JANNATUL BAQI**. It is where Imam Hasan, Imam Sajjad, Imam al-Baqir and Imam al-Sadiq are buried. Many of the companions of the

Prophet and members of his family are buried there too."

"That's more Imams and special people than any other place we've been to so far!" Zahra said. "What are we waiting for? Let's go and visit the shrines and send our salaams."

Grandfather didn't move.

"What's wrong?" she asked. "Why aren't we going there?"

"There are no shrines or mosques there, and we are not allowed to go near the graves," he said in a quiet voice.

"How is that possible?" Yasser asked. "There's always a shrine above the grave of an Imam...isn't there?"

"There used to be mosques over their graves, but many years ago," Grandfather paused to try to count the years. "About a hundred years ago, these mosques were destroyed."

"Why?" Zahra asked, creasing her forehead in concern.

"Oh, for many reasons my dear Zahra. You have seen from our past adventures how threatened the enemies of the Ahlulbayt have felt because of their greatness."

"But what excuse could they possibly use to do such a terrible thing?" Yasser asked.

"They said they were worried that people would worship the graves," Grandfather replied, unconvinced.

"Wasn't it enough for the enemies to oppress the Ahlulbayt in their lifetime?" Zahra asked. "They still continued to oppress them even after they were martyred."

"The guidance of the Ahlulbayt is so powerful that even their memories can change people and make them turn towards Allah," said Grandfather. "That is why they were chosen to be our leaders after the Prophet and that is also why their enemies feared them even after they killed them."

"It's not fair!" protested Yasser. "We need to do something!"

"Sometimes we don't have the power to change situations ourselves, but there is a day dedicated to commemorating this oppression and calling for change," Grandfather explained. "It's called **YAWM GHAMM, THE DAY OF GRIEF**. We commemorate it on the 8th of Shawwal. In the meantime, we need to continue to pray for the day when we can visit them properly."

"What we need is Imam Mahdi to come and help us fix this," Yasser said, determinedly.

"We can't just expect Imam to come and solve all our problems," Zahra said. "We need do to our best as well. We have to show Allah that we are ready to serve and obey our Imam through our actions every day."

"That sounds like a very good plan," Grandfather said. "For now, let us turn our hearts to the holy personalities buried here. They can see us and hear us and return our salaam.

A lump rose in Zahra's throat as she looked at the flat land of Jannatul Baqi; it looked like an abandoned construction site. The grandsons of the Prophet were buried here without even proper markings for their graves, while his mosque stood in honour next to them. How sad he must be to see how his children were being treated.

Yasser saw her face and came to stand next to her. "I know it's sad, but we have to always be positive and trust Allah, right? Prophet Ibrahim did all the things he did out of love of Allah and look at how Allah honoured him by making everyone who goes for Hajj copy his actions. We know the Ahlulbayt also did everything out of Allah's love so maybe we can honour them by following in their footsteps and copying their actions too?"

Zahra looked at her brother as if he had just shared the most precious secret. "You're right, Yasser!" she cried, with tears in her eyes. "You're so so right!" She gave him a tight hug and whispered a fierce "Thank you" into his ear.

Yasser shrugged in embarrassment and tried to get out of her hug, but it was a half-hearted attempt. He didn't mind Zahra's affection, but she did choose the most awkward times and places to show it. When she let him go at last, Grandfather turned them all to face the graveyard and recited the ziyarah aloud with the children following the words after him.

Then they sat in the courtyard of the mosque enjoying the serene Madani air. As the breeze grew cooler, the shadows grew longer and the colours began to turn into golden shades of the evening, they knew it was time to go home. This time, even

Grandfather seemed reluctant. He raised his hands in prayer and asked Allah for the opportunity to visit Makkah and Madina soon. He opened the Qur'an once again and recited the verse that had started them off on this adventure:

"CALL ALL PEOPLE TO THE HAJJ. THEY WILL COME TO YOU ON FOOT AND ON EVERY LEAN CAMEL FROM EVERY DISTANT PATH, SO THEY MAY OBTAIN THE BENEFITS IN STORE FOR THEM…"

"What an amazing journey we have been on!" Zahra said, thinking about how much she had learnt. "All these millions of people answer Prophet Ibrahim's call every year."

Yasser was thinking further back to the du'as they had recited in the month of Ramadhan. It finally made sense to him that when they had been praying for the opportunity to go for Hajj, what they had actually been praying for was the opportunity to get closer to Allah. Even though he had not performed the Hajj for real, Yasser felt that he had truly experienced the benefits of Hajj.

They all stood up and faced Masjid al Nabawi for one last look.

The rug beneath their feet rose and hovered for a few seconds before **WHOOOSH-ING** forward and taking them back home.

Chapter 27

DING DONG!

"Grandfather? Yasser? There's someone at the door!" Zahra called from upstairs.

DING-DONG! DING-DONG! DING-DONG!! The insistent bell complained.

"Okay, fine! I'm coming!" Zahra ran down the stairs, wondering where her brother had disappeared to. She couldn't find a hijab and grabbed a clean tea towel from the kitchen to cover her hair instead. It was probably a delivery for something Grandfather had ordered online, so she opened the door just a crack, thinking to grab the package and rush back in. To her surprise, she was met by Mrs. Muntazir's puzzled face.

"Salaamun Alykum," Zahra said respectfully, very conscious of the striped cloth wrapped around her head that she was holding in place with one hand.

"Alaykum salaam, my dear!" Mrs Muntazir replied. "I haven't heard from you in a while so I thought I'd come and check in on you. I did promise Mum that I would keep an eye on you all while she was away. What have you been up to? Are you baking a cake?" She looked pointedly at the towel.

"Yes...I mean No, I'm not....yes, we're well alhamdullilah..." Zahra was flustered, both touched by Mrs. Muntazir's kindness and embarrassed by her state. "Please do come in." She opened the door wide to let her in.

Mrs. Muntazir stepped in carrying a heavy dish wrapped in foil. "I made you some vegetable lasagne. You must eat your greens even if your mum is away!"

"Oh, thank you!" Zahra took the dish with a smile, now using the kitchen towel to hold it. She guided Mrs. Muntazir to the kitchen. Just as she was setting the dish on the counter, Grandfather and Yasser came in from the garden where they had been planting tomatoes.

"Oh, Mrs Muntazir," Grandfather said warmly, as he removed his boots and put away his gardening gloves. "Salaamun Alaykum! It's lovely to see you. Welcome, welcome. Let me make some tea for us."

Mrs. Muntazir asked the children about their school and how they were coping as Grandfather made the tea. When it was ready, they all sat around the kitchen table. Grandfather placed a steaming cup of sweet vanilla-scented tea in front of each of them and a plate of cookies and cake in the middle. They continued to chat as they drank the warm, milky tea.

"When is your mum returning?" Mrs. Muntazir asked.

"On the twenty sixth, inshallah!" Zahra replied.

Mrs. Muntazir looked her watch. "That's in just three days. You must be so excited."

"We can't wait to have her back!" Yasser said. "I heard that when a person comes back from Hajj, they are as clean as a newborn baby, with all their sins forgiven!"

"That's true," Mrs. Muntazir said, nodding. "Your mother is very lucky."

"Hajj is a wonderful spiritual journey of the heart," Zahra said dreamily. "I wonder how Mum felt going round the Kaaba, performing her saee and stoning the Shaitan. She must have felt so connected to Allah and also with all the other Muslims as they copied the footsteps of Prophet Ibrahim and Lady Hajar! I can't wait to hear all her stories."

Mrs. Muntazir was speechless. "I had no idea that you knew so much about Hajj!" she said, delighted. "Have you been reading up on it?"

Yasser's eyes widened and he looked from Zahra to Grandfather, not sure how to respond.

"Ah yes!" Grandfather cleared his throat. "We have been trying to learn all about Prophet Ibrahim and Hajj so that we are prepared to appreciate Mum's experience when she comes back."

"Well in that case I'm sure you want to give her a proper welcome home!"

"Do you mean with a **PARTY**?" Zahra asked, clasping her hands in delight.

"That's exactly what I mean! Prophet Muhammad said that we should have a walimah, a meal shared with family and friends, on five occasions and one of them is when a person returns from Hajj. You can do something to show your mum how much you have learnt about Hajj. I'm sure she will be impressed!"

"That's a great idea!" Grandfather said. "Mrs. Muntazir, would you be able take care of the invitations? I can prepare the food and Yasser and Zahra can organise some party games."

"That sounds like a plan," Mrs. Muntazir said with a nod.

Chapter 28

BEEP BEEP BE-BEEP BE-BEEP-BEEP

Zahra had already woken up before her alarm for Fajr started ringing. Today was the day that she would see Mum again after so many weeks! Happiness and excitement filled her heart, but she was also a little nervous. Would Mum be a different person? How much would she have changed?

Zahra rolled out of bed, turned off her alarm and made wudhu. As she sat on her prayer mat facing qiblah, Zahra tried to remember the feeling of being united with all Muslims around the world, facing the same direction and praying to one God. She remembered the prayer of Prophet Ibrahim for a nation of people that would worship God. *Please let me be part of the answered prayer of Prophet Ibrahim*, she pleaded in her qunoot.

As Zahra's mind raced between excitement to see Mum and the reflections from her amazing adventure, her thoughts drifted to Lady Sarah. Zahra could clearly remember the look of yearning on her face, and she wondered whether Lady Sarah ever had any children of her own. She opened her Qur'an to read her morning recitation, (Grandfather insisted on them reading at least five verses, with the English translation, every morning). Yesterday, she had read verses about the people of Thamud and remembered her time with Jamal and Naqah fondly.

She asked for protection from Shaitan and began in the Name of Allah before opening the Qur'an to where she had bookmarked her last reading. Her eyes scanned the page as she read familiar names in Arabic, "Ibrahim..." she whispered to herself. She could not wait to find out the meaning and her eyes shot over to the translation:

"AND HIS WIFE WAS STANDING BY, SO SHE LAUGHED, THEN WE GAVE HER GOOD NEWS OF [THE BIRTH OF] ISAAC, AND, AFTER HIM, JACOB."

She gasped and held the open Qur'an to her chest. "You are so generous," she whispered to Allah with tears in her eyes.

In the room next door, Yasser pressed the snooze button on his alarm for the second time. He had been up till late planning the party games with Zahra and he was still very sleepy. He wearily rubbed his eyes and forced them open to look at the time. The first thing he saw was the post-it note he had stuck onto the face of his bedside clock. It said: "**SACRIFICE YOUR SLEEP**!" in large bold letters. He remembered how Prophet Ibrahim was willing to give up his own son to be closer to Allah. *I can sacrifice a little sleep to wake up for Fajr*! he said to himself, jumping out of bed and heading to the bathroom.

Grandfather had been awake much earlier than either of the children. He had recited Tahajjud prayers up on the roof garden and then made his way down to the kitchen to begin preparing the food for the walimah. Grandfather took great pleasure in feeding people and he wanted to make sure all his dishes turned out well. He rubbed the meat with spices and garlic before placing it in the oven to roast slowly. Next he began preparing the saffron rice with raisins and pine nuts. For dessert, Grandfather decided to make Zahra's favourite, warm chocolate brownies with hot fudge sauce and vanilla ice cream.

Grandfather carefully placed a bowl of chocolate chips on top of a saucepan of boiling water. As he watched the dark brown spheres melt, he thought of how Prophet Ibrahim had always cared about all people. Prophet Ibrahim would look for people to share his food with and never ate alone. He never gloated at other people's misfortune and continued to pray for his uncle even after his uncle disowned him.

The Qur'an shares that when some guests came to visit Prophet Ibrahim to tell him about the punishment they were going to inflict on the people of Prophet Lut, Prophet Ibrahim offered them food, not realising they were angels. When he realised who the angels were, he pleaded to them to save Prophet Lut. He was loving and caring to all people. He was known for being Haleem, tender-hearted. Grandfather silently prayed for a soft heart that could love and care for all people.

Mum's plane was not arriving until four o'clock in the afternoon and Mrs. Muntazir had insisted on picking her up from the airport. "Imam al-Sadiq said that the person who meets one who has returned from Hajj and shakes their hand in welcoming them back is like a person who rubbed his hand on the Black Stone!" she had told them excitedly. "Please let me have this reward first!"

Naturally they had agreed, because it also gave Yasser and Zahra enough time to decorate the house and get the party games ready.

Yasser popped his head into Zahra's room. "Do you have any sticky tape?" he asked. His hair still standing up from a good night's sleep.

"Yes, I think there's some in this drawer...have you finished wrapping the **PASS-THE-PARCEL**?" she asked, rummaging through her stationery drawer.

"Allllmost! Just a few layers left," he replied. "You know, I feel like the whole of Hajj is like a pass-the-parcel." He was feeling pleased with all the comparisons he was suddenly finding to Hajj in his daily life.

"I know what you mean! It's like every time we stopped, we unwrapped a layer of understanding!"

"Yeah, and under each layer of wrapping in our game, we've explained something about Hajj!" Yasser said. "That was such a good idea!"

"Mrs. Muntazir is going to love that! Ah, here's the sticky tape!" Zahra handed it over to Yasser. "I still have to hide the clues for the treasure hunt, but here is a draft of the map. What do you think?"

She handed over a crumpled, tea-stained paper to Yasser. He inspected it for a moment. **"SAEE – THE SEARCH,"** he read out loud, scanning the paper. "Do you think our guests will find it too difficult?"

"Well, it wasn't easy for Lady Hajar!" Zahra said, remembering how Lady Hajar struggled but kept her trust in Allah (swt). "But I can add in a few more clues."

"Perfect!" Yasser said. "That just leaves **THE MOVING MUSALLAS!** I'll get the prayer mats ready. Can you ask Grandfather for a recording of the adhaan?"

"I already have! He has it on his phone."

"Nice one!" Yasser was impressed with his sister's organisation.

"We've got all the games sorted, but I don't have a clue how to decorate and we don't have much time. Any ideas?"

"Hmmm, how about we make a welcome home banner," Yasser suggested. "And balloons are always fun!"

"Yes, let's do that!" Zahra exclaimed. "I can't wait to see Mum!"

"Me neither," said Yasser. "Grandfather said to expect them to be home by five. We've got lots to do before then!"

Chapter 29

The doorbell started ringing at around 4:30 p.m. when the first guests began arriving. The teachers from the Islamic school arrived first to see if there was anything they could do to help. Next came a few of Yasser's friends and he welcomed them, taking them to the living room.

"Why are there lots of prayer mats on the floor?" Ammar asked, looking around in surprise. "I've been your neighbour since forever, and I've never seen so many prayer mats on the floor!"

"It's not even time for salaah!" Salman added.

"It's for one of the party games! Moving Musallas!" Yasser told them.

Ammar couldn't contain his laugher. "And how are we supposed to play that?"

Yasser explained the rules of the game and they played a quick practice round before everyone else arrived. The boys ran around the living room pretending to be busy in their daily lives. Ammar pretended to play video games while Salmaan pretended to play football with Maytham; kicking around an invisible ball was more fun than they thought it would be.

Suddenly, Yasser switched on the adhaan, and the boys had to run to the closest prayer mat. Maytham was the first one out, he was having too much fun dribbling the invisible football to hear the adhaan being called! Each time they played, Yasser removed one prayer mat from the floor until they were left with one winner.

"That was fun!" Ammar said, slightly out of breath. He had thoroughly enjoyed himself. "You're right Yasser, we're so busy in our daily lives, but when Allah calls, we should answer straight away!"

"And it's not just for salaah," Yasser said, thinking about all the pilgrims who had answered the call first made by Prophet Ibrahim. "Allah calls us to do many other things like struggling against Shaitan and going for Hajj." Yasser remembered how the pilgrims had sincerely responded with "Labbayk – I am here! O Allah!" The only words wajib to be recited during the whole Hajj.

Zahra scanned the living room. "Is Maryam here yet?" she asked, looking for her best friend.

"Not yet," whispered Grandfather, "but I'm sure she'll be here soon. Can you check on the brownies for me in the meantime?"

A tantalising aroma wrapped around Zahra like a warm hug when she entered the kitchen. The air was thick with the scent of roasted garlic and herbs mingling with the sweet perfume of caramelized onions. She carefully opened the oven to check on the brownies and was immediately met with a wave of heat and the sight of sticky chocolate. *It's almost ready*, she thought to herself. She decided to wait in the kitchen to take it out and remembered how her mother had stood in the exact same spot just a few short months ago, telling them that she was getting ready to go on a trip of a lifetime.

Maryam arrived just as Zahra took the brownies out of the oven and returned to the living room. Zahra ran over to give her a squeezy hug. Maryam had brought some flowers and a hand-made card for Mum, which they set down next to the gifts others had brought.

"You must be so excited to see your mum!" Maryam said, knowing how close Zahra was to her mother. "What have you been up to? You haven't called for ages!"

"It was pretty tough," Zahra agreed. "But we had some great adventures here too with Grandfather. Did you know that you can experience the benefits of Hajj from home too?"

Zahra's statement piqued Maryam's interest. It was one of the things that Zahra loved most about her best friend; that Maryam was so curious and had a thirst for learning just like herself. It reminded her of Prophet Ibrahim and how he questioned everything around him. The girls sat on the stairs and Zahra told Maryam about their adventure. Maryam was amazed at Prophet Ibrahim's life.

"When you first started talking about Prophet Ibrahim, I thought that God must not like him very much because bad things kept happening to him…"

"Those were tests," Zahra clarified.

"..and through each one, Prophet Ibrahim got closer to Allah (swt)?"

"Yes! It was because he passed those tests that Prophet Ibrahim became a role model for all people. He showed us all how submitting to Allah is the most important thing. And you know what, Maryam?" Zahra looked her friend in the eye. "Prophet Ibrahim expected Allah to help him through all his tests, he relied on Allah alone and he was ready to be happy with whatever Allah decided for him. That's what helped me when I was missing Mum. I prayed to Allah to give me strength and He helped me so much!"

DING-DONG!

There was something different about the way the bell rang this time, and Zahra quickly looked at the clock – 5:10 p.m. Her heart skipped a beat. She ran to the door where Yasser was waiting to give her the other end of the banner. They stood behind Grandfather and held it out together as he opened the front door.

WELCOME HOME, MUM!

More of Yasser and Zahra's adventures
Available from: www.sunbehindthecloud.com

www.ingramcontent.com/pod-product-compliance
Lightning Source LLC
Chambersburg PA
CBHW030036100526
44590CB00011B/226